POSTSCRIPT

Michael Krüger

Translated by Karen Leeder

The Sheep Meadow Press

Einmal Einfach first published by Suhrkamp Verlag in January 2018.

All inquiries and permission requests
should be addressed to the publisher.

The Sheep Meadow Press
P.O. Box 84
Rhinebeck, NY 12572

Designed and typeset by Sheep Meadow Press
Distributed by Syracuse University Press

Library of Congress Cataloging-in-Publication Data

Names: Krüger, Michael- 1943, author. Leeder, Karen- 1962, translator.
Title: Postscript: New and Selected Poems
Description:
Identifiers: 978-1-937679-88-0(pbk.)
Classification:
LC record available at:

Acknowledgements

Thanks are due to the following magazines who published some of these translations: *Areté*, *No Man's Land*, *PN Review*.

I

III

I

"All my poems
are occasional poems,
they are inspired by
reality and find their
foundation in it."

Goethe to Eckermann

POSTSCRIPT TO A POETICS

For Alfred Kolleritsch

1

Poems are mistrustful,

they keep what has to be said to themselves.

They go through closed doors

into the open to speak with the stones.

They make off with us.

When we want to catch hold of them, they say:

check against promised delivery.

Everyone knows they write us out of existence

with a few forgettable, oblivious lines.

Once I read a poem

about clouds, an itinerant folk.

It was pouring with rain. And from below,

where the pond was slowly filling up,

I heard the grizzling of frogs.

2

I'll steal a word from every month and take it

on my grand tour into the heart of waiting,

almost six hundred words, my whole life.

Some of them I can no longer find,

they have slipped inside letters, hidden away,

impossible to deliver.

3

In Krakow, not so long ago, in memory
of Czesław Miłosz, evil came into the language,
the way it does these days, in a poem or
in some other disguise.
Someone from Gdansk, once known as Danzig, had seen it
as a woman lay dying, in her pain.
The weather in Krakow was splendid.
The Tuchlauben market bursting with people
and Mary with the little lamb
took utmost care to keep the peace.
Evil was abroad, that much was clear,
but whenever you tried to grasp it,
you felt the touch of a poet's sleeve
and had nothing in your hand.

4

At some point in time every poet
tries to write a poem about water,
about waters or water itself,
off his own bat.
Not like the great painters
that had a different brush for every wave,
a pupil for the rushing brook,
and a master pupil for the sea,

skilled at painting the wave as it breaks

and nothing else. You had to feel

the hunger of the sea, its voraciousness.

Things are more difficult for us.

Some didn't get past the prayer,

others attended to the rhythm of the waves.

Even still water that shows our reflections,

was and is an image of horror.

Someone in a great poem declared

that water has no memory and no history,

he should have listened to it for longer.

5

Theological Questions

A man is sitting on the steps in front of St Anna,

his yoghurt pot half-full of coppers.

He has rolled up the legs of his trousers

to reveal his wounds, or what

used to be his legs.

He claims immortality, begs for money

with these words, says others are dying his death.

The young folk in the cafe across the way

have no desire for revelation.

They have no clue what lies ahead.

6

First of January, Resolutions

I am starting a new notebook
for questions that need no answers.
How long will this snow
linger on the rowan twigs?
Last night I dreamed I was riding
the wrong way on an escalator.
I wanted to find the returns depot.
My use-by-date had passed.
Why this unbearable reticence in me?
And why, as recent years,
does the stone have no voice?

7

The clouds are racing, as if there were an ultimatum,
and oak branches where the wind loses its way
are beating the air in despair.
From the schools of stillness,
with their highly elevated windows,
scarcely a glimmer of light falls on the path.
Knowledge is no longer beautiful,
it no longer moves us.
Ah, you far-sighted clouds!
Somewhere children are playing,

you can hear their excited shouts.
And suddenly a ball spins up to
my feet, and a child orders:
join in!

8

I took the sleepy paths
down to the lake in order to escape the post.
For days now the postman has been talking to me
about Last Things: the scent
of pussy willow after rain,
our memories' allegiance to truth,
and that one should not, for Heaven's sake,
keep pestering God with
reason. In the midst of this torrent
of words he hands over obituaries,
black-rimmed cards with Rilke's verses
on existence or quotations from Benn.
It is finished:
our generation is taking leave.
Which lines from our poems
will make it into the great anthology?
The lake lay before me like molten wax
calm and languid and without depth,
like a childhood dream of happiness.

NIKOLASSEE, BERLIN, FEBRUARY 2015

They say I grew up here between

our local church and Kleist's grave,

two holy places for our higher endeavours.

Sheep would graze on the Rehwiese meadow,

but how were we to speak with the shepherd

who only understood the language of lambs?

You are leaving the American Sector,

though none of us knew which way

the hare was going, the wind was blowing.

Here, on warm summer afternoons,

we would dream of reaching into the spokes

of the world in a brotherly way.

Above us a large cloud and another, smaller,

mother and child, nothing else needed.

My parents' grave is already up for sale,

how quickly the wheel has turned.

BERLIN, CITY OF CHILDHOOD

At the end of the street, just
where it curves,
so one cannot see
whether it goes on,

sits an old dog.
He clearly doesn't know
how to get home.
It's like that with me.

I was quite certain
that I lived here once.
In the house opposite
a bomb was once diffused.

A young woman brings her
rubbish to the bin in triumph,
as if it contained her whole life.
Out with it. She observes me for a long time,

but comes to other conclusions.
From an open window the sound
of a crying child.
It must have been this house.

HOW IT WILL NEVER BE AGAIN

I'd like to smell wild cumin again,

soaked in vinegar water;

see the scaly clouds over Kayna;

listen to flies

singing their funeral dirges on the window pane;

observe the shadows that creep round the house

and cast the book of life into darkness;

feel the bright light, the eyes of God.

There where I stood abashed as the sun went down,

red as a cockscomb.

What did you say? Nothing. I just dropped

something beyond the Seven Hills at the back of beyond

where Europe ended and my childhood began.

MY GRANDMOTHER

expected neither reward or punishment

from life, she knew exactly

what wasn't at stake, the rest was

for men in uniform

or philosophers.

Gloves, for example, she

never wore, so as not to make them dirty.

Chamomile, cornflower and broad bean

went to school with her,

all of them passed with Distinction,

as there were no fertilizers

after the great war.

What splendid broad beans.

Here, in the mountains my grandmother

never saw, when I looked today

at the grey grass from last year

that could finally breathe

after the long siege of winter,

I was reminded once more

that she expected neither reward

nor punishment from life.

But what, then? Nothing,

truth be told, nothing.

GRUNEWALD

For Markus Barth

1

The frost that strangles the birdsong;

and my words too, only yesterday a key to the world,

have suddenly fallen silent.

A blue tit at the window is looking at me

like a Tibetan monk. Tweet, I say,
God has not done right by you birds.
You can practice and practice and never
manage any kind of song.

2

I am open to visits. The A19 comes to a stop
right in front of my house. Everything I do
will turn against me.
Sometimes I open the windows at night
and listen to the darkness. It borders on torture
when voices enter the house
but you cannot see the speakers.
No speeches at the graveside, please, pious hope.
Scattering the ashes into the eyes of the lilac
before the wind takes care of them.

3

In the hall of my apartment there is a mirror that knows
more about me that I do myself. A specialist in kindness,
every day I fall for its tricks. Its oracles,
its own defenceless laughter! You should live, it murmurs to me,
simply live, I ask nothing more. And I: but I want
to see myself, I scream at it, I want to have seen myself
once in my life, is that too much to ask? Be still, it says soberly,
in four weeks we will be living apart again.

INSTITUTE FOR ADVANCED STUDY, BERLIN

For Lucia Giuliani

The little lake opposite, that greets me every morning
is part of a larger one, connected by dark arteries.
Like an eye that harbours slumbering dreams at night
while language recovers from knowledge.
Bathing forbidden. Miserable willows guard the banks
and ducks, heads bowed like monks,
agitate the standing water.
Steps lead down to the lake from the sleepy villas
with their damp cellars, the shadows of previous owners
leaning against the walls. Sometimes I see people
standing there with strained smiles, as if they knew
that nothing, in truth, belongs to them.
The sun seems proud of this lake,
only birds don't honour the rule of silence.
One wants more from life than life is prepared
to give, so runs the motto of our institute.
Our boss is an archaeologist: he knows a thing or two about that.

INSTITUTE 2

I have to leave now. The cleaning crew

is at the door so that the bed can be prepared

for the new guest. I leave behind

one empty future, two dozen books

that can't hold my attention, a hairdryer

and hundreds of papers in the rubbish bin

covered with symbols with which I hoped

to outwit silence.

The birds that woke me every morning

will remain, the black stream, witness

to my failure to dedicate a poem

to melancholy, the sycamore, acacia trees, dust.

Even the light I leave behind, the stillness

and shadows in the empty rooms.

Life, they say, is warmed by death.

Is that true? A clean sweep can begin.

PUZZLE

Garden tools, empty flowerpots, a scythe without a grip

and a nameless stone, that I picked up,

God knows where, just in case it was needed.

A shadowy world, dry and still,

the quiet alphabet of happiness.

Two splinters of mirror on the garden table:

one shows the man I no longer am,

the other the man I can no longer be.

Between them squats misery with its thousand eyes

that see everything, even what does not exist

and never will.

EUROPA

I am still a bloody layman

when it comes to telling

the world of good from that of evil.

It is all much easier.

As I was going home today

I saw the children playing Europa,[*]

with all of those beautiful unsaid words

that are in vogue.

A grey sky, offering no comfort

lay across the city, but as I

paused by the linden in the yard

I heard the chorus of roots singing.

* Europa: A children's game akin to hopscotch

FRESH SNOW

Overnight snow
on the trees. The courtesy
with which it touches twigs,
then books, your eye,
your stammering heart.
It takes a long time to understand childhood
for even snow knows shame.
I don't know where to look beneath the white,
and what I find are stones that turn red
when one touches them courteously.

ROTTEN TREES

When at last the shadows had gathered
before my eyes and within them,
and the shadow of the yew had surrendered
itself to the shadow of the sycamore, and the poor roses,
almost invisible now, had been sent to seek
another heart for the night,
I saw how a light had surrounded the trees,
a silvery sheen like rotten wood.

If the linden tree is not mistaken
and it rarely is, at this age, tonight a storm
will come and seize us all by the throat, one
that has no pity for rotten trees.

THE PINE AND THE SYCAMORE PLANE

The pine tree that must compete
with the sycamore in the struggle
for light, has bolted.
No one in this district has the time for it,
here they like leaves not needles.
Ivy has it in its grip
and will finish it off before long,
I hope.
I've been watching this tree for years
as it reaches for the sky,
and the sycamore does everything it can
to set itself apart, in a good light.
I cannot decide whether
I should prefer one over the other,
both of them block the clear view
I enjoyed in their youth.
I need vistas, open space, perspective,
now there are green sentinels before my eyes
that measure their lives against mine
which, of this they are both quite sure,
will be shorter than theirs.

CHILDISH EXERCISES

Take the grass, the helpless grass,

in your hand before you cut it.

Or, as a gnostic exercise, place the stone

back on the wound left

in the earth. Or look, with a thinking eye,

at a placid surface of water that does not recognise you.

Or, more difficult, approach the angel

that stands at the door and cannot decide

whether he belongs in the house or outside.

Or listen, quite simply, to the sound

of footsteps on frozen snow.

Or imagine a world without you and without

others – observe, in other words,

the dark side of the world with the wonder

of a child, so as not to run straight

into the arms of comfort, before any atonement.

THE NUT TREE, TIME

The nut tree had to have faith that
its longing for order would be stilled.
Ten years ago I set a bare root
into the earth, an austere stick,
three years later the first nuts,
puzzling fruit, supposed to be
the likeness of our brains.
Everything is sacrificed to order:
childhood, youth, the garden, sorrow.
My brain alone has remained
as disordered as that unruly nut tree
that cut the ground from under the hazel.
But I needed its shade,
a place to rest and observe,
at the expense of truth, for all I cared.
The empty space is now home to misfortune,
in whose shadow time has made its home,
rapacious time that seizes all for its own,
above and below the earth, in broad daylight.

THE GRAVE

Look, the shining seam
of our steps, leads to the grave,
as if the moon had split in two
and bitter, cold and bleak, shone down
on our path alone wanting
to know nothing
of the life in our bodies.
Let us lie next to one another.

My hunger is already given over to the roots,
my thirst to the stones,
my words to the tiny creatures
that make ready for us a bed for the shortest time.

ANOTHER VERSION OF RECORDED HISTORY

Wind drops. A dog slinks past,
does not grace me with a single glance.
It leaves behind a path clearly marked
in the snow. The birds are reading earnestly
the beechnuts that lie black
on white: don't make things too easy.

From far off the cry of a siren,

a sound for charming snakes.

As if this quiet were not enough

to imagine another life.

THE EVERYDAY

Whenever I fetch the morning paper

my own life suddenly appears to me

like someone else's hasty sketch

in the Miscellaneous section.

The newspaper is heavy,

as if the bad in the world had weight.

History consumes itself,

soon there'll be nothing left

but headlines.

It is becoming more senseless

to believe in a sense to it all

that weighs more than the Miscellaneous.

If it weren't for the apple tree

in my garden, I'd throw in the towel.

8 MAY 2013

Unless I'm very much mistaken
God has hidden in my apple tree.
For the first time in years He has
chosen this tree above all others,
not exactly an upright specimen
of its kind, with woody
bitter-tasting fruit. But the bees
love it. When I lean, barefoot,
against its trunk, and eavesdrop
on their stories, there is
humming talk of a sea of honey
that even Moses cannot part.
I can hear God laughing.
Then even the birds keep their beaks shut…

IN THE COUNTRY

Who says that the heavens
are empty and that the man who cowers
beneath them under the scrutiny
of the stars is world-poor?
On the doorstep, at home,
lies the passport of the dead,
brought in by the cat.

Now take an elder switch

to beat the demons into flight

that crouch under the doorframe,

as if they lay in wait for you.

MARCH 2014, UNDER THE APPLE TREE

This is the hour of those who know all,

who, in spite of all reason, go

searching through the ashes for bits of proof

that they themselves have burnt.

Disappointed pedagogues.

But the wind takes the ashes,

the wind that consumes all, scatters them everywhere,

over believers and unbelievers,

over the beehives that are falling silent,

and over our dazed hearts

that beat on tactlessly into the emptiness.

The ancient art of withstanding contradiction,

in order to experience the incomprehensible face

of beauty has been forgotten, like many a skill,

or is superfluous, like the right to be amazed.

I sit idly under the apple tree

listening to the monologue of the branches

and watching the holy shadows

as they prepare for dying,

long before sunset.

2015

It's supposed to be the year of fat bumblebees
the year of plush linings, of high time,
of warmth that rises from frost and fog,
the year of wide skies and clever books,
that dream of the future in the shadows,
the year of bees and honey.
It's supposed to be a long year of spiders
that knot their silk tighter round my neck,
the year of poor words and the mouth
that warms them. It's supposed to be: a year.

AUTUMN 2015

Night creeps through the grasses
on bare feet
colours the apples black.

Autumn has tipped
great tubs of grief
onto the garden
and none of it will
drain into the earth.

Migrants, empty rucksacks
slung over their shoulders,
carry the cold through the land.

One of them passes a photo around
of the sun over the ocean.
Since he has been on dry land
the sun is nowhere to be seen.

WALK IN MAY, 2016

The sky a grey basin of ash,
where a greedy wind buries itself.
The earth steams with early warmth, beckoning
roots towards the light. I shall stop being a child,
shall not ask the grass for advice,
when the stones withdraw and are silent,
as if it really were a question of life and death.
Something else is at stake. It cannot be spoken
in my language. The dead know it:
they argue night after night in my head,
until morning switches their voices off.
Here and there patches of snow
that will not disperse, and on the weir
the complete works of old leaves.
But for the angry sobbing of the wind,
the truth might make itself known,
the artless truth that looks so much like grass.

LE MONDE, JANUARY 2017

For Yasmina Reza

A flimsy, miserable morning

after a long, wretched night.

With honey in my veins I circle the house

like a cat, the wind leans against the gate,

and the sycamore takes pains

to tickle the grass with its spiky shadows.

What should one serve? The truth

and the people. But a man is never

who he thinks he is and, in spite of your work, the one

who comes home is not the one you expected.

He is already inside the house, preaching indifference,

holding forth as if he's out on the square, ice

rattling in his words. There'll be no light now:

we can't find the switch that must be thrown

before we go under.

The little man across the road

with the lantern he hoped was lightning

to make the world legible

like a book.

IN THE ENGLISH GARDEN, MUNICH, JANUARY 2017

An angry shaft of light across the snow

like an endless scream

that darts across the unfamiliar world

as if a fever were breaking out.

If you look down from the weir onto the river

the stones at the bottom look like a type case

of memory, blurred in a flash

by a swarm of minnows to form new patterns.

How often I have stood here,

on the suicide bridge, with the grinding hum

of the city at my back and stared at the water

that seemed to me to be time itself.

Out of the blue the crows gave their blessing.

IN WINTER

In drifting snow I lay,

by the larches, where in Autumn

the wind gathers the sheep,

just waiting for the end

of distraction. No more birds

in the rowan, no sound,

no hub-bub in this white state.

Inscrutable and empty.

Eyes closed I saw
my grandmother's chapped hands
as she skilfully quartered an apple
and made us all equal
on a winter afternoon.

THE SITUATION

We have been robbed
but we don't know
what is missing.
We come home,
heave a sigh of relief.
The thief, whom we know,
keeps his secret:
he wants to spare us.

II

"The idea of travel
is bound up with
arrival. But does
one truly want to
arrive?"

Günter Metken

JUST ONE-WAY

It is good to travel through
Germany by train,
always running too late.
You're in no hurry.
Allotments creep
round the cities
like snails.
At the end of your life
you're given the gift of a day,
that you can fritter away
at the railway buffet
together with pigeons and sparrows.

AUTUMN AT LAKE CONSTANCE

November. The maize still stands
like a stiff brown wall
and takes up my whispering.
No word out loud, no shout,
just a niggling doubt: will the sheath
hold the bright yellow grains.
Radical unbeliever, is it that
which unites us or sets us apart?
The maize speaks all languages.

High above Reichenau island where

writing came into the world, a kite circles

and the books – that always insist they are

in the right because otherwise they would

cease to be and death would have to

stand by watching as we disappear

into the maize – the books stay shtum.

HOTEL ROOM IN HANNOVER

The room is empty.

The pigeons on the window ledge

speak Russian for beginners

before they're poisoned.

A bed is moved in,

it shines in the dark;

then a chair, water, pencils,

that remind you of novels.

No sense in a lamp.

The export-experts are asleep,

do not disturb. This season's must have.

A tourist group from China

wanders through the heating,

looking for the internet.

On a bench in front of the hotel

a pipeline is being tapped,

Russian oil, conspiratorial blackmail.
Across from the station
at 5.12 the escape-bid succeeds,
with all the unwritten books.

NIGHT SCENE

The station has already departed;
only the train tracks still remind
you of dealings with people.
Body rubbed with salt,
goat skin over the shoulder,
we search between the tracks
for the blue yonder that has gone inland –
not out of compassion,
but duty. All the clocks
are armed to the teeth
and hobble after time.

ZBIGNIEW HERBERT'S CHAIR

One day in March 2014, in Warsaw,
I get the chance to sit in Zbigniew's chair.
Sun is shining through the bare branches
of the sullen trees in front of his window,

not letting the dust come to rest,

above the books, a solid wall

of philosophy and art history

in five languages. Did he know this cat

sprawled in front of the Greek classics?

With his spidery hand he filled his books

with scribbled notes: everything is so different from

what they say it is, his shaky words say,

that follow the crooked path of history

into the bright heart of beauty.

And then Herr Cogito comes into the room,

his voice wheezy with smoke,

sits down on a new chair opposite me

and speaks about how religion vanishes

in theology. We need a lifetime,

he says, to understand what a stranger

will grasp at first glance – that we are

just as insignificant as all the others.

Herr Cogito smiles. Darkness comes quickly.

Soon Warsaw is a city of dark once again.

AT THE EDGE OF THE PATH

Follow your path
the uneven one,
I'll wait here,
where mint and honeysuckle
cover the cross.
I have an open heart,
the ants march through it,
I can feel their legs.
They are making off with my heart
with wonderful industry.
The masterpiece of the meadow,
in bright colours and the cross
that cannot be seen
with the naked eye.
When you come back
you will no longer find me,
but the cross will tell you
where I was.

CLUJ, HOTEL BELVEDERE

Still the mist keeps the churches hidden from view,
but I can hear their Roman Catholic murmuring.
I too keep myself ready.
The ambulance drives the night's deceased
home to the land beyond the forests in safety.
When the pigeon shadows brush the dogs
the lights go out and the world becomes more graspable.
In the breaking light I also see
the garrulous mafia of sparrows.

BEFORE VIENNA AND IN VIENNA

Amiable clouds, like farmers, selling their wares
at the market, accompany us into the centre.
The city does not intend to save my life.
In the hotel room stands a wall of words,
I translate them half-asleep.
I don't know what side you're lying on,
but I can hear you breathing.
When I strike a match
darkness leaps into the room:
we must not let ourselves be seen in Vienna.

IN THE SOUTH, BY THE SEA

Gorse and other prickly plants, the same school,
frugal companions, that manage without water for weeks,
but are spic and span in the wind, surrounded by insects
that rise and fall as if drawn on threads
above the green sculpture. What paradise looks like?
The world is so chock-full of misery that song
had to be invented, even though it's not a solution.
There is no solution, not even writing.
Sometimes a wave breaks over the cliff
and leaves behind a little sea on the path
for a few seconds and the strange smell of water
and warm dust. The horizon is darkening
and reveals the impossible thing that resists
words, those disloyal adjuncts. Now is the time
for ants and their teeming whitewash.

DREAM OF 27 SEPTEMBER, MODENA

In a garish coloured leaflet
displayed in the hotel,
there was a description of the city
to which I had been brought.
It did not have a name.
In glowing footnotes

it spoke of donkeys

whose braying could be collected

to guard against fever and diarrhoea.

The bill, and as always, no receptionist in sight.

VICTIMS

In the cathedral at Modena, a glittering temple

of prayer, birds at home on the roof,

move the pale stones to tears.

Every dark hand received small change

and with a clink I deposited the rest in an

offertory box that thanked me in Latin. Wait there,

an old man called after a child; I waited.

I was pleased not to be ashamed.

After the service I lingered outside a long time

looking at photos of victims, partisan soldiers,

pinned to the North Wall,

with the names and dates of their brief visit

on earth. Some had a cigarette hanging

from their mouth, all were staring at me.

A wall of staring faces, that accompanied me

back to my hotel, Libertá, Best Western,

just behind the synagogue, where soldiers guard

the lament, as they do all over Europe. We must send
God back to school, I thought. In a corner
of the tiny room a spider was working away
at its thread, undaunted: it is high time.

3 OCTOBER 2015

On the day of German Unity
I was sitting with Maimonides in Córdoba
in a cafe behind the synagogue.
He spoke with dignity and grace
on the subject of tolerance, scarcely audible
among the chattering tourists.
I was waiting for a call.
At our feet a dog lay panting
for a name. You, my dear dog,
belong to a people without writing
that struggles against hunger and ignorance.
All those in the café were on their phones
as if they wanted to know more about one another.
Maimonides was silent.
Gradually life ebbed away, but so slowly
that the hope dawned that a future might be
imagined before death.

HOTEL VILLA POLITI, SYRACUSE

In front of room 130, the entrance

to the underworld, tiny birds

keep watch at the gate,

which is itself invisible.

It is so dark

that one might easily grasp

exactly who one is.

At midnight the tour guides are ready,

they accompany you through the honey

of memory, a tough business.

Then you hear the dead whispering,

they are obsessed with the question

of why the living want to stay alive.

At the end of the corridor a faint light,

that is where Saint Lucia is buried.

Even she had bad breaks,

like all of us, who lack the right words

for a pact with the devil.

LOW FLIGHT

Like a graveyard, that's how the airport looks;
still thirty interments to go before evening,
in Toulouse, for example, in Abu Dhabi and Berlin.
And the queue for Belgrade or Izmir is long.
Do you remember the graveyard at Izmir
with the best pistachio ice cream, the best in the world,
and the living seemed like the dead in disguise
who had forgotten what language to use
to speak to us? Last call for Herr Hatake,
who is expected at his grave in Paris, but
is queuing for Münster for an urn burial.
With every ticket you get a little hourglass
made of plastic, the sand has run out by daybreak.
Some people hold it skew to try and cheat time.
Dreadful music from all the loudspeakers.
And where once the Vienna coffeehouse stood,
one can now pray, together with the dead.
I spy my neighbour from Warsaw in the queue,
she has a written a big book on the praying mantis,
that is fated to consume its mate
although it tastes of nothing.

BEAUTY

Today in the train from Krefeld to Cologne

an old woman was passing from seat to seat

offering beauty.

Everyone stared out of the window

so as not to have to look at her.

She had heavy, tired hands,

with a ring on each finger.

Hands that believed in eternity.

Her story is one that everyone knows,

even if they cannot understand it.

What if the gift is refused?

A shrug of shoulders passed through the compartment.

And the old woman, beauty in her hands,

shuffled further along, through the train

and then on outside, as there were

no doors in the last car.

The train stopped, we had to wait

for death to pass through on the other track:

he was running late. Six minutes.

But approaching Cologne, the speaker announced

we will have made that up, no trouble.

Have a pleasant journey!

PESCARA, IN NOVEMBER

The sea washes letters onto the beach
franked with snow, secret
messages for the time
after death.
The wind rages in the palm trees.
My little pencil sticks
with me, the rest makes off
into simplicity, that yearns to be free
of all description.

EASTER WALK

The way back across the water, along by the gorse
that steals wool from the sheep.
A ship draws the sunset
across the water like in old legends.
The dune grass stirs as if something were afoot,
and the lizards about to proclaim it.
The gorse is home to the gods, they are hungry.
I am the leader of irresolute souls
but I may not turn round.
Before me the ancient olive tree, the judge,
with his thousand salty eyes,
he has the path in his sights that divides the waters.

A god without feet, I thought,

that cannot run for the hills like me,

must contemplate misery for a long time,

and only when the sun has skedaddled,

can he become my companion

on the long journey home.

HOTEL KANET

At the window of the Kanet Hotel in Skopje

I suddenly saw the white butterfly

I knew from home fly past. I refused

to believe it had followed me,

on the long, dusty journey to this place,

but its technique gave it away:

the nervous fluttering and sudden stillness

sitting on the heads of the generals

that lined the streets with iron determination,

as if there were more to command

than the brown leaves of chestnut trees

that already in June hint at Autumn.

It danced at my window like a puppet

recounting its journey.

The police in Innsbruck had waved it through,

the Serbs, Croats and Albanians had stamped its wings,

a Cyrillic visa on white silk.

I sat mute on the bed and looked at it.

The heat and the din of a rock concert in the park

Was bothering us both.

The dancing white font on his wings was easy to read

in the fading light.

With his last strength he reaches the cypress trees

that watch over the hotel like Cyril and Methodius.

In an hour he will be a scrap of white

in the mulch under the trees and the mice

will take pity on his soul. Dear cabbage white,

how could I ever forget you.

IN SKOPJE, 2015

Night, the hour the heart stands still,

the room next door is empty.

I am the only guest and listen out

for the ottoman mumbling

about mulberry trees.

Am I now old?

Wrinkled arms, worn-out hips

and liver spots all over my skin,

together they form a puzzle:

join the dots in the right way

and death is the jackpot.

Outside the window a match

is struck: will it illuminate the world
or disappear in flames?
Next morning a conversation
moves in next door, in whispers.
I didn't understand a thing.

IN MACEDONIA

In Macedonia, in the evening,
you enter an inn back to front,
so you don't see
how you are welcomed.
The linden trees follow you
across the threshold, even the bees
are permitted in the bar.
The tables are scattered with books
that know each other by heart.
Behind the bar hangs a mirror
with an image of Alexander the Great
falling off his horse.
Take water with your Aniseed brandy.
It dissolves the honey in your heart
before the infarct.

IN ABRUZZO

From the birds-eye view
that I love, the fly in the ointment
cannot be seen, the Calle Pineto,
where the massacre took place
seventy years ago. Black moths
emerge in the light
of the fire, freed
from inertia and history.
What we say has been sensed by the dead,
what we know, we know from them.
We must
say the words over, like lost children,
in order to stay alive,
the Calle Pineto leaves us no choice.

IN CASO DI EMERGENZE

for Anwar M. Shaikh

one may not use the lift.
But there are steps missing on the stairs
and families huddle on those
still intact telling anecdotes
about the beauty of the clouds.
A strange hotel, without a roof
and without the flaw of perfection.

The storm presses for a statement of fact.

But, as always when one ends up here,

the heavens suddenly tear open

to reveal, on a washed-out clearing

the inauguration of the Council of Swallows.

GREETING THE FRIEND

After a long absence

you return

to us, your impoverished relatives.

We recognise you

by the deftness of your hands,

the way you hold the fork,

and the serrated knife.

When you look at things

they blossom, as always.

Your project in the world at large,

the codification of everything,

is not complete, even if you talk

as if the future were all used up.

We grow smaller and smaller

as you speak of the great story,

your head leans against the wall,

like someone not from here

and for certain not from there.

SHEEP

for Caspar von Lovenberg

Yesterday I found myself thinking again of the sheep

in Mezin. I had got out of the car

and was gazing across the gentle slopes of Gascony,

that are so invitingly gentle, and thought to myself

life has nothing to top this:

these swelling waves of wheat, barley and sunflowers

that once were headed for the ocean, when the world began.

Not everyone reaches the sea.

Suddenly with the sun at midday and no shade,

I found myself surrounded by a herd of sheep.

They want to crush you with their woolly closeness,

I thought to myself and a sheepish fear

crept through my body in gentle waves.

But they took me in, protected me,

I became a sheep and so I have remained.

Some people want to be a running dog with flying ears,

others a cat, and nothing else will do.

As for me: I'm a sheep, a sheep among sheep,

a valued member of the flock.

AFTER THE FEAST

The tents had been dismantled
and we were stragglers in the early morning.
The empty meadow after the feast
watched over by lindens with shepherds' souls.
The stones slowly growing cold.
Can you prove who you are?
Take heed, warned the words,
before they were silenced
by the reaper's scythe.
What was never really real
cannot be deciphered.

BY THE WATER

To sit without stirring
by the waters, a brook.
All reasonable arguments
float by, nothing lingers,
the water will not give in.
The smell of pine needles
and young nettles in the heat.
A sorrel leaf in your mouth
to forbid any laughter.
The greatest misfortune still is

that we cannot hold our tongue.

All that one has never been.

A gleaming express train

that is never late

when it is permitted to run.

Stay sat here, be silent,

do not borrow words from the water,

let them go their own way.

Stick to the stones,

if you have a hankering to speak.

SUNFLOWER SEEDS

Sometimes I ask myself

whether we will see one another again,

the Madonna with the ermine in Krakow,

for example, or the sunflowers in Laroche,

that hang their dried-out heads

before harvest-time, no strength

to turn towards the light.

Ryszard writes that the Madonna

still wears her worried face.

I remember her differently,

bright, like a sunflower in the morning.

So I remember a different life,

a different past,

that begins long before harvest.
The seeds of the sunflowers
from Laroche can be bought,
three Euros for a little bag.
One must split the husks,
spit out the rest.

FLIGHT

The sky is full of vapour trails,
as if the gods were being hunted.
They give it their all, soundlessly,
and dissolve, without beginning or end.
A deafening silence
in which drones feel at home,
freighted with Christian values.
In the plane all around me
enemies that were once friends.
They have mastered the art
of blotting out misery.
Drones fly ahead of death
to ensure it meets no resistance,
before we land in the here and now
and evaporate.

III

"The transcendental face
of art is always a form of
prayer."

John Berger

MODELS

Please, take a leaf out of the book
of bees. Each individual comb
is equally filled, even in winter
there is enough for all. Do you hear,
nonetheless, how they hum
the song of imperfection? Our world,
queen or not, came into being
through language, each word
born on the tongue, released
from the mouth into the familiar. Bees
translate and the wind, creeping
round the house like a thief, gathers
them in and makes a line of verse:
that all we have to do is repeat.

IN THE PARK OF MUSIC

for Alfred Brendel, with all my heart

The gate is always open, anyone can come in
and leave behind a sound in the gravel,
terror and war are welcome too.
Anyone that comes bearing a knife or a pistol
must face blackbirds, sparrows and doves
that fly after the planes when it's noisy.

The children love the din too, they want

to catch the sound with their open hands.

And then suddenly it falls so quiet

that one can hear the flies lamenting

and my book switching languages in silence.

In the furthermost corners of the park where,

against the iron statutes of time,

darkness has taken up residence like old grass

Schubert is turning the creaking wheel of longing

as if a world still existed that had need of him.

BOOK OF LEAVES

The sun that has just shone through

the topmost branches of the sycamore

and is reading a page from the Book

of Leaves, that knows no beginning

and no end, warns you to make haste.

In each leaf the centre is present,

even in the last one already hanging in the dark.

The wind is reading along too, it skips a page

while the woodpecker insists on a full stop

and the finches mix up the lines

so the folksong cannot be sung

in the old style.

THE BEAUTIFUL HOUSE

for Wolfgang Rihm

Nothing in this house belongs to you,

that much stands in Gothic script above the door,

licked by ivy and vetch, loved

by bees and midges too.

On this bright day

the key has gone AWOL

sleeping in other locks.

The sycamore is an old master,

giving his gifts to the wind,

and the smell of lilac hunkers

in the hedge, which stands hunched

an anthology of love poems

that no one reads any more.

This is where free will is supposed to reside,

when it is not going door to door,

selling itself at knockdown prices

or so says your neighbour, wrapped

in his coat of stone.

If you press your ear to the door,

you hear the ticking of a clock,

loud enough to wake up time,

so that death who is idling under

the apple tree, picking thistles

out of his heart, has work to do again.

DEVOTION

Underneath the motorway bridge

a church is being built

out of rubbish, an old pram

serves as the altar.

Words of forgiveness and

grace. Memories

that are no longer needed.

The vicar is ancient

and usually drunk.

But he has got into God

and everyone listens

devotedly as he

curses the world.

RHETORIC

After sundown, we heard,

Demosthenes would hold a lecture

in the quarry outside town.

We were there, also those

for whom it's all as clear as mud,

when it comes to the truth.

He picked up bits of gravel

and put them in his mouth,

to make his tongue smooth.
When he said care or complaint
a stone leaped
from his lips.

At the end, his mouth empty,
he swallowed a fast-acting poison.
Sleepy and irritated, the audience
made their way home.
I hung back, gathered the tears
before they dried.

SUGGESTION FOR POETRY READINGS

You have to speak quietly,
always quietly,
so not everyone can hear you.
Press your lips together
so the truth has its hands full.
Listen to the city breathing.
And never raise your head,
So as not to look misery in the eye.
Every explanation of misfortune
means an increase in wretchedness.
The inner puzzle needs few words,
you can say it more succinctly.

SHADOW ECONOMY

The trees look like gallows,

their leaves shed after the storm.

Under the tree a gaggle of people

burying their passports

as they have done since time began.

Shoes thrown onto a heap,

who needs shoes?

The clock hands are taking their time:

the time I need

to escape from the image.

SNOW

I touched the mantle of white

and under the mantle two warm countries,

Rich and Poor, in my frozen hand.

Has the story reached an end?

Under the snow the ice is waiting

to bring you, broken, into the valley.

OF THRONES AND CHAIRS

Wasn't it only yesterday
that we were all lying on the ground,
I mean the whole of humanity,
considering
how that man there, him on the throne,
could be brought to silence?

And today we all sit on chairs,
I mean the whole of humanity,
considering
where the fear comes from
of having a story that can be told
without a pause.

THE RETURN

The fly, a moment ago,
that stumbled across the table
as if it needed to recover
from a great weariness.
Between the breakfast crumbs
it was reading what had been left behind,
the spoiled remains.
People who wander over garbage mountains

and know everything about us. Everything.

They do not know the vow of poverty.

Later, already at my books,

I saw how the fly retraced

its own steps and died.

WHITETHORN

That's enough swooning about sunsets,

where the air over the sea becomes so thin

that it cannot hold a butterfly.

Enough about crows standing around in puddles

like people that don't have a clue what to do

with their money. Never again mention:

the formality of tulips, the rusty red

of the lichen and the yellow of dried-out moss,

the colour of the oak tree bark in the rain

and willow stems that shake their fists.

No more of all that.

What does it cost for the upkeep of a soul, inflation adjusted,

of course, but cash in hand just the same?

Or is everything free?

Look how the upstart whitethorn imposes itself.

SUNFLOWERS AND POEMS

See how the sky vaults
above the disgruntled wretches who dig
their claws into their little patch of earth
and turn their gaze from the light,
while the sunflowers
turn on their own axis,
without twisting their grey necks,
to capture the very last ray of sun.
There is a kind of poem
that allows you to hide,
and others that reveal you.
The mirror hanging in the shed
has become unfaithful over the years:
it does not capture the light any longer
that I use to express myself.
If things carry on like this
it will soon be harvest, oil and poems.

LIFE A DREAM

I don't want to dream any longer,
now that night after night the room has started
filling with all those people that once,
fleetingly, crossed my path.

My path. How that sounds —

a handful of gravel I managed not to stumble over.

They stand round me and stare

as if I had deprived them of my life.

Go on then, spit it out!

Since I haven't been sleeping

more of them have come.

They write down what I say,

and send it to me registered post.

I read. And understand nothing any more.

Is that meant to be my life?

EVIL

Today in the city, in the second

That one casts no shadow,

evil stood suddenly before me.

At last eye to eye.

A breeze, abroad by chance like me,

blew dust into my eyes,

and when I opened them again,

my shadow leapt ahead.

I still had my hand raised

to paint graffiti curses,

as children sometimes do.

THE ARGUMENT

The argument had two hands
that would not let go.
So departure turned into
staying behind. Hope kept itself
dry under an umbrella.

THE MAN FROM EIBISWALD

I live here in this house,
I was born here and
hope I will die here too.
Sometimes I ask myself
how time passes.
I like talking to time
but it always wants to move on, on.
My favourite colour is green.
Jacket, doorframe,
doormat, wellington boots:
all green, even the umbrella.
How many different greens
exist in the world?
Once I loved all colours
as one can see from the rag rug
lying on the bench:
all my own material.

I know that I am alive

but I cannot explain it.

Sometimes when I'm sitting here

on my bench

an unhappy shadow flits

across the wall, because time

will not stand still in a place

where everything else is at home.

BIZARRE, BUT TRUE

When I sit on my terrace at night

with the starry sky above me

and language that resists turning into law

under my tongue, I look up,

full of mistrust, at the sabre-rattling stars

that watch over our Cold War.

Some of the twenty million or more

that step out of their front doors like me,

key growing warm in their hand,

give themselves away,

others stand around on the stunned earth,

smoking in silence and freeze.

But nobody knows what to do

on a starlit night like this

that gives us reasons to be alive.

HOUSE ON THE EDGE OF TOWN

Dame Care has built herself a house
on the edge of town, the place for those
who don't know where they belong.
The house has no windows.
She lives there with two old virtues.
Patience and Gratitude,
that lay the cards for her of an evening
and a toothless dog.
The Fool does the shopping:
lightbulbs, wire, plaster for gout.
Sometimes an old man comes round
to help in the garden, you can hear
his joints crack as he bends down.
Dame Care's cucumbers, he says,
taste of cucumber, as if that
were a truth worth pointing out
No one has seen Dame Care for many years
and some people even wonder
whether she is still alive.

REVERIE

Nothing to be hoped for
as the heavens are already silent
and the land crumples
without resistance.
Expounding laws, changing them
to correct the status
of the sun, everything
is obliged to change
until waiting is worthwhile.
What burns alone is the voice
that once had authority,
the familiar tone.
We want to honour the dead,
the guardians of yesterday.
Take the dust with you
for they love dust,
give the dust over to ashes,
from which everything grows,
that keeps us human –
without them we would be nothing.

DAILY EXERCISE

for Friedmar Apel

Like a schoolboy I sit
before my tree, the teacher.
A lesson lasts twelve seconds.
The tree instructs me
in the art of shadows, silence,
what it means to be upright.
If the wind attends us
school is out
and work can begin.
Beauty is buried
under my tree,
but digging is useless: you can't
see it, you must say it instead.
A woodpecker gives out grades:
failed again,
God be praised.

ENTRY FORBIDDEN

I live in a town called Unrest.
In the supermarket an icy substance
trickles through the body
and disappears into the earth,

without leaving a trace.

It will cost you all that you are.

The people in my town

wear old prophets' cloaks,

wolf on the outside, sheep within,

good for the soul.

A dripping roof gutter serves

as a clock, we don't have much time.

We make tea each day

of cornflower and celandine.

When the fever abates

the flowers droop their heads,

it is time to talk to the stones

that bear responsibility in these parts,

as if that were a job of work.

GOOD INTENTIONS

It's dusk, I still have an hour

to offer the daylight a few lines

under my own steam. It is so quiet

you can hear things starting to whisper.

Misery grows in the distance, where I,

chained to proximity, am not,

but wanted to be, when I was young.

It grows more patiently than one can imagine.

Time to make plans for the time before,

to try to give the cause

that we call life, a direction,

a good one, we hope, that would be the thing.

But the depths do not draw me,

not while I can watch the birds

sketching a house in this late light,

without care and without tears,

a house where one can live well,

a house for pilgrims without rancour.

THE OTHER GOD

When, out of the blue, one becomes as old as I am

one dreams ever more frequently of a country

devoid of the hoax that is sold to us

as life: a different kind of tale.

The whole business with God, too.

For example, the notion that behind our God

there is another, to keep God in order,

is unsettling. Keep God in order is not quite it,

or not exactly, in any case. The fact is

that our God has lived too long in the hope

of not being seen through. But because all men

need something to fear, they should not always

be forgiven. That is the truth.

With these thoughts in mind I sat under the tree

and watched as the days went inland,

sometimes gradually, then all at once,

as if they were in a hurry to get away from my thoughts.

FLY

Today, eyes wide open, I followed

the fly who described every centimetre

of the window with untiring patience,

behind which spring was starting to stir.

I thought that its crazy serif scrawl

would be read from the other side

as a great poem about the comfort

of failure in a too generous world.

At some point, in its broken verse,

it fell onto the window ledge and waved

its tiny legs, as if it wanted

to finish its uncompleted work

before the end. Then the dawn

wiped the window with a rosy gesture,

because a life that promises nothing

may have no end rhyme before death.

HOW I SPENT THE NIGHT

Where should the other world begin,
the foreign realm where sober voices
meet no resistance, and simply give up
just as we all give up, when evening
wears on and need knows no way out?
We never turn wise, that is the law.
The crickets know it, and the glow worms
that gleefully empty their batteries.
This tree by the lake, a refuge for me
for a long night, bedded down on liverwort
and stinging nettles that smell of dull heat.
I hear how the bats scrape the water
and force the fish to change their element.
And, if it hadn't been for the shrill cry
of a night bird, carved as if from stillness,
I would have lost my belief for good.

VICINITY

By my bed
stands a lion.
He must live nearby,
because he visits
regularly,

73

once a month.
When he is there
I sleep peacefully.
No bad dream
dares to show itself
in his vicinity.

FLIGHT OF FANCY

Misery squats
on mattresses spread
in chaos round the room.
A bottle of wine does the rounds.
Outside ships pass
but cannot lay anchor.
You can hear your heart
before it bursts
in the quiet.

15 MAY

I have made a little fire
in the garden to find a halt
in the flames, but it will not burn.
My gaze follows the clouds of smoke

that struggle up from the ashes

and tickle the nut tree, the Naysayer.

How should one remember

what the grass whispers.

Even the woodpecker stutters

when he tries to write the word grace,

this wonderful one syllable word,

with five letters.

A village close by is called Unrest,

armed shadows live there,

all paths lead to it.

I want to master the gift

of never forgetting

the best things in life,

but there's no mastering gifts.

NOTHING THAT WE KNOW ALREADY

We live from those moments when the storm is over

and we may become part of the ground;

when day and night open up at last,

and let us back in;

when a certain light lies over things

like a cloth that slipped away from the swallows;

when the larch rises from

the tear in the web and teases the sky;

when the woodpecker with the dark look

dictates his monotone we can talk about anything

to the beeches that guard the possible

in the cool realm at their feet.

Nothing we know already: that's what we live from.

Insight, discrimination, joy and memory,

they shall be ours, or so it is said in the final testament,

but only if we remain children, who get on the wick

of the world, before it burns out.

ABOUT PHILOSOPHY

We must proceed from the assumption

that predictions do not come true,

something always goes wrong. Always.

There is no relying on people,

that's why we are still alive.

One man looks out of the window

and follows a dog with his gaze,

another admires the light

on the bright leaves of the linden.

Too many are only for themselves

and not for the cause. We have a sense

of our boundaries, no more.

History, says a friend,

is the science of human misery.

from Leopardi to Cioran.
The poetry of imperfection,
the bond between philosophy and mourning,
that is our task: for
humans are hesitant creatures -
are they not?
Come on, let us walk, walking
helps us to understand the everyday
without having to translate it.

ELECTION SUNDAY

Nothing new to be said
of the clouds, their silent company,
they seem to rest over the land.
No longer peace and not yet war,
even the spider knows this. Only yesterday
busy in the hedge occupied with
the wide-meshed story of summer,
now it sits in the corner of the window
and waits for sun.
No more butterflies,
that make the blood stand still in my heart.
And the apple tree? Shrugs its shoulders
as if ashamed that this year
it cannot fling a single apple

into the dreary green of the lawn.
It looks more and more German
in old age. Nothing new to be said
of the clouds since Goethe,
They hang above the land
in which bondage is seeking
retribution from freedom, as it says
on the placards that will be
packed away again tomorrow,
to make room for a clear view
into this dark land.

OPEN WINDOWS

Some of them hunker back to back
with their lacklustre books
brooding on revenge.
Evening passes by
simply plucking the dead
from their open windows.

Everything we see

is given a name.

Even the stars

that dwindle from lack of light.

They keep strictly

to the path of the comets,

the pilgrim's route

that ends at a shimmering

harbour: the Pleiades.

Only here,

in this state within a state, do we go without names.

Even the moon,

by an indissoluble destiny,

bound to us,

can offer no help.

It has no biological value.

Surrounded by its stars

it is the very ideal of intransmutability.

A cold king in a kingdom of connections.

Craters and mountains, ground punctured

like a sieve.

From that distance

life seems a little less important,

or so say those who come home

by the light of the moon,

with dry feet, because it draws

the water from the earth.

OBSERVATION

Someone has chiselled
his name into the cloud
above my house
with bloody hands.
Everything that passes
turns red.
Quickly shut the windows
to keep the colour inside
that is not red.
And please don't ask to read.

REQUIEM FOR A WIND

Not so long ago words stood here,
albeit embarrassed and full of shame,
and here and there one of them was broken.
The world too small for their ambition,
for a grand new beginning.
The world wants other words,
since sheer amazement
has found itself in freefall
and does not need the good old words
to celebrate dumb gluttony.
Then a wind came up, from nowhere

that would not let us sleep,

it had grown fat on war,

on a thousand sorrows,

and let false misery dance.

It was over before daybreak.

And, shaken to the core, art went to gather

all the losses, for which there was no language.

Only pictures.

IN THE FOREST

Sometimes it seems to us

that we might still lead

our lives towards a goal,

not death, but something before it,

that, in truth, shares a common root

with death, but deviates from it

with most precise pedantry.

The rain has stopped suddenly,

but the trees keep dripping for hours.

If you were simply to stand,

rooted to the spot, would you know

what remains to be done: a little,

a lot, or even the one key thing?

But you want to go on, even if you

are obliged to love life,

and are suddenly counting drops

as they fall to the damp earth.

The forest takes pains

to look like a nineteenth-century painting,

in which people are forbidden.

The inventory of the sky is empty,

the stars all cashed up.

I wanted to show the child

a shooting star, the most exquisite

soundless game invented by a weary God.

Perhaps there is nothing to wish for?

Perhaps we already live in paradise?

NOTEBOOK

He wrote in his notebook:

How smug are those who survive!

They have drawn the pain from the future,

the sweetness from the honey,

the thorn from the thistle.

Suffering does well in solid houses,

we can hear it lumbering about at night.

A great noise without quiet survived.

It stands above the market square and cries.

IV

Missed Opportunities

for Manfred Trojahn

1

The way she stood there, explained the man
from Rome, leaning against the wall,
with eyes long since drained of joy,
as delightfully languid as a day
in late summer and as forbidding
as the enterprising little gods
that kill time at the Pantheon,
time that wants no truck with humans,
and the way she raised her right hand,
slowly as if the air were thick with syrup,
and touched her face, a dusty vista
of parched fields and arid springs,
in the hour in which day separates itself
from shadow and the sounds of Rome
start up once again, I was suddenly certain
that it is her we have all been waiting for
at the end of a long present
that will not cease to be.

2

I sat in the café, a woman says, alone,

not far from Ostia, right by the sea,

enjoying that emptiness that comes after joy

and reading your postcards scribbled to the very edge

with all your faithless words. A ship put out to sea

led from the harbour by screeching gulls, it took

my memories with it and left me empty behind,

unfathomably empty – save for my childhood,

that refused to go; the scent of overripe figs,

inconstant love, inadequacy, all that stayed with me.

The bridge from desire to action destroyed.

Even yesterday I thought these postcards from you

would last me a lifetime, this gloopy kitsch,

more viscous than any great confession.

A man sat close by, two tables away,

he seemed familiar, but not enough

to stir my memory. His flat face

a blank slate, ready for an open word.

3

On one of these hollow-cheeked days
in November in Berlin, he said,
when the sundial can only count to three,
and the city tries to sleep
under a sheet of fog, I sat on the bus
that crawled down the Kurfürstendamm
in the outside lane, the road surface glittering
like a runway of broken bottles.
Schlüterstraße, Bleibtreu-, Fasanenstraße,
familiar corners, Benjamin-country,
now clogged with fashion and fast food,
so that, if misfortune wins out, wishes
can be fulfilled. That's when I saw her,
wrapped in a raincoat that ballooned at the back,
her gaunt face like a Käthe Kollwitz etching,
bent over a map of the city, searching
for the horizon, that we as school children
still believed lay in this cast-iron quarter.

4

It started to rain, she said,

and in Hannover, if you know what I mean.

I was sitting in the hotel across from the station

gazing at the faithless trees that buckled

awkwardly as if they were in pain.

Beside me in the lobby on an ugly little chair

sat a young rebel in his coat and asked his grandmother:

so was your life worth it, then? And looked at me

incredulously, as if he could not quite believe that he was

the instigator of such tastelessness. Sitting there

just like his father, I thought, who has passed on his idiocy.

I was just about to spoil his day with my scalding coffee,

when outside I saw the man go by, the one

I had been waiting for, the one on whose account

I had come to Hannover for the first time in my life.

He looked strange, too much soul for his body,

wretched. In any case, I thought, as he got into a taxi,

I ought to have footed the total bill.

5

A conference forced me to travel to Warsaw,

he complained, though I would have preferred Lisbon,

especially on the anniversary of the earthquake.

We had arranged to meet in front of the castle,

not really a good idea, as ten thousand couples

had gathered there, parading their bliss,

and would not be parted, on any account.

It could have been worse, I told myself

between two phases of abject despondency,

when I couldn't find a trace of you.

In the next church I came to I lit a candle,

just the one though, so as not to spoil Mary,

for one thing, but nor to provoke death,

that was also present. It came to me kneeling in the pew,

that I thought of you as I would a dead person,

I saw your restless face harden into a mask.

I had come to the point where the life

in me was creeping back into lifelessness.

6

In the hotel across from the cathedral
in Barcelona, she said, I had taken a room
right at the top, in order to wait for you.
The mirror was blown and a fly that did not know
it would be dead by nightfall, was trying
to read me the future, then gave up.
Even the mirror did not recognise me.
On the steps of the cathedral, in bright sun,
the unbelievers were praying and squabbling
over a coin dropped by a bird, one of those birds
that have been trying for centuries to raise the cathedral
heavenwards. Smoke filtered up from the drain,
doubtless Zurbarán's lamb roasting down below,
and beside it an old man pouring his heart out
to the excited sparrows. A column of ants
crossed the balcony, it must have lost its way.
Then I saw you come out of the chapel
and disappear into the crowd.

7

No idea why we should be meeting in
Stockholm, of all places, in February,
when you can't see your hand in front of your face,
but she insisted on a 'cold' conversation.
Three long days I sat in my hotel room
and watched as the snow dissolved without
trace in the harbour basin. The future of man
is uncertain, were her last words on the telephone,
but we have a good chance of survival.
She loved the idea of the liberation of the world.
On the fourth day I got caught in a demonstration
at the cultural centre. If she were in the city,
I would find her here, though I was not sure
I would recognise her, we had missed each other
too many times. That night I saw a TV report
about the demonstration, and did not understand
what it was about. But I saw myself in the crowd
and behind me, he, mouth open wide..

8

It was one of those crazy ideas of his

that we should meet on the night train to Venice.

I got on at Munich and went to the dining car

so he would be able to see me. One seat was free.

I sat opposite a bag full of blood who was laying cards

in order to read his fate that was already written

all too clearly in his face. In the dark I could hear the panting

of a herd of buffalo racing past us; it was chasing a moth

that went ahead opening the borders. Of the man supposed

to be waiting for me, no sign. In Austria the beds left the train,

they were needed elsewhere, and took their dreaming with them.

We had to sleep standing up like destitute thoughts.

Every word that went through my head helped to build the wall

that kept us apart. There's nothing left to be said about Venice.

On the way back I saw him on a vaporetto

chugging towards us, hair flying in the wind.

He flicked his years into the water like coins

and did not even look at me out of the corner of his eye.

9

For the tenth anniversary of our missing one another
we wanted to meet in Saint Germain, in Café de Flore.
I got there early so as to take the furthest
corner of the veranda and observe her arrival
as she picked her way between wolves and sheep.
Europe was drinking overpriced coffee,
as if nothing had happened. Our common earth,
I read, that shares no kind of communality any more,
will go to the dogs, still shooting off at the mouth
Only we will survive, together with this fly,
shamelessly cleaning itself on my plate.
Don't be afraid, I whispered, I'll stick with you.
That's when I saw her. She stood on the other side
of the street and seemed to be wondering if it was worth it.
A beggar held out his hand towards her and she
rummaged in the pockets of her coat for a long time
looking for a coin that she handed over so clumsily
that it fell to the ground. Then she disappeared.

10

In the end it was Sils-Maria, unavoidable in a way.

It was June, she said, and one could feel

how the world set itself against the changes.

The Gregorian chant of the falling drops

and on Nietzsche's stone a first timid moth

with wings clenched, that would not fly away

before it was ready. Here I sat, waiting, waiting,

for nothing. Beyond good and evil, enjoying

first the light, then the shadow, all just play,

all sea, all great midday, all time

without aim. But no one came down from the mountains.

In the forest cabin on the Chasté peninsula, no guest

that resembled him, no footprint in the mud,

just this moth that must have once seen him.

A crippled bird limped past, head high,

ducks on the lake gleaming like ebony.

From time to time I heard whispering voices,

that cut through me like a knife through bread.

I was not surprised she wanted to meet me in Jerusalem,

she loved clichés and stones. The day will come when the stones

will speak to us, was one of the things she used to say.

She loved the clear shadow of the tamarisks,

the solemn donkeys at the Gate of Mercy,

weighed down with a burden as old as the history of mankind,

a honey messiah with a pine-needle crown,

a God who lost the key to his creation.

I asked after her in the American Colony, in the King David, too.

No one knew her name, no bed had known her body. I had

slipped through all the churches like a cat, had given myself over

to the singsong of the many languages, born here in the sand, the prayers

and calling and laughter of the birds that circled like drones

above the holy places and the lost souls in the evening.

Then I saw her. She stood in the courtyard of the Armenian Cathedral

where the decayed skull of the apostle James is housed.

She stood wrapped in a white shawl, with a priest in the shadow,

that grew denser and denser until at last the Sabbath began.

12

It was harder that expected to find him again, she said.

First the snowfall filled his visible tracks

then a desultory rain, and in the end the wind

worried at our paths until they could only be glimpsed

from far away. Now and then I found a photo of him

in the newspaper, black and white his gloomy face,

a panorama of misery. In the cities I sometimes

ran across his shadow that reared up before me,

and must have been on my tail. And I heard him,

it must already have been spring, skulking through the fallen leaves,

the leftover foliage, like an obstinate child

that can no longer lift up his feet. And then I found

a note from him, written in copper plate,

under an empty wineglass: Back soon. Please

don't wait. That was in Skopje, in one of those noisy cafes

just behind Alexander the Great's horse,

where one doesn't notice time making a fool of you.

But it made a fool of the two of us, him and of course me too.

13

I had to learn to walk past her
without stumbling, or returning her gaze.
Sometimes I saw her sitting in a café,
playing with a book in front of her,
as if it had nothing more to tell her
or as if it has lost its voice.
She looked shabby, tired of life,
just her shoes with their customary shine,
they, she sometimes said, would bear the brunt
of death. Just bear it, of course, not accept it,
for she had outlived the fear of death.

And that's how I could imagine her as dead,
a last wakeful dream in her face,
already cloaked in the night of the world.
The last words must be spoken by the eyes,
the slow alas, as if dipped in honey.
We will meet in some place that is nowhere to be found,
she said, where our voice is waiting for us.

The cycle 'Missed opportunities' was written on the suggestion of Franz Xaver Ohnesorg and was set to music (wonderfully) by Manfred Trojahn. The pianist Hanni Liang played at the premiere on 16th July 2017 in the Lehmbruck-Museum in Duisberg. I offer heartfelt thanks to all three friends.

EINMAL EINFACH

I

»Alle meine Gedichte
sind Gelegenheitsgedichte,
sie sind durch die Wirklichkeit
angeregt und haben darin
Grund und Boden.«

Goethe zu Eckermann

NACHTRAG ZUR POETIK

für Alfred Kolleritsch

1

Gedichte sind mißtrauisch,

sie behalten für sich, was gesagt werden muß.

Sie gehen durch geschlossene Türen

ins Freie und reden mit den Steinen.

Sie führen uns fort.

Wenn wir sie aufhalten wollen, heißt es:

Es gilt das versprochene Wort.

Jeder weiß, daß sie uns wegschreiben

mit wenigen vergeßlichen Zeilen.

Einmal las ich ein Gedicht

über Wolken, das wandernde Volk.

Es goß in Strömen. Und von unten,

wo sich der Teich langsam füllte,

hörte ich das Quengeln der Frösche.

2

Ein Wort aus jedem Monat nehme ich mit

auf meine grand tour ins Warten,

etwa sechshundert Worte, mein ganzes Leben.

Einige kann ich nicht mehr finden,

sie haben sich in Briefen versteckt,

die als nicht zustellbar gelten.

3

In Krakau kürzlich, zur Erinnerung
an Czesław Miłosz, kam das Böse zur Sprache,
wie es sich heute zeigt, im Gedicht oder
in andrer Verkleidung.
Einer aus Gdańsk, vormals Danzig, hatte es gesehn
im Sterben einer Frau, in ihrem Schmerz.
Es war herrliches Wetter in Krakau,
die Tuchlauben quollen über vor Menschen,
und Maria mit dem Lämmchen
gab sich alle Mühe, den Frieden zu wahren.
Das Böse war anwesend, das stand fest,
aber immer, wenn man es greifen wollte,
hatte man den Ärmel der Jacke eines Dichters
am Wickel, also nichts in der Hand.

4

Irgendwann versucht jeder Dichter,
ein Gedicht über Wasser zu schreiben,
über Wasser oder das Wasser,
eigenhändig.
Nicht wie die großen Maler,
die für jede Welle einen anderen Pinsel
und für den eilenden Bach einen Schüler hatten
und für das Meer einen Meisterschüler,

der die Welle malen konnte, wenn sie bricht,

sonst nichts. Man mußte den Hunger

des Meeres spüren, seine Unersättlichkeit.

Wir haben es schwerer.

Manche haben es bei der Anrufung belassen,

andere den Rhythmus der Wellen belauscht.

Auch das ruhige Wasser, das uns zeigt,

war und ist ein Motiv des Erschreckens.

Einer behauptete in einem großen Gedicht,

Wasser habe keine Erinnerung und keine Geschichte,

er hätte ihm länger zuhören sollen.

5

Theologische Fragen

Einer sitzt auf den Treppenstufen von St. Anna,

sein Yoghurtbecher halb gefüllt mit Kupfer.

Er hat die Hosenbeine hochgezogen,

damit seine Wunden freiliegen oder das,

was einmal seine Beine waren.

Er sei unsterblich, mit diesen Worten

bettelt er um Geld, andre sterben meinen Tod.

Die jungen Leute im Café gegenüber

haben keine Lust auf Offenbarung.

Sie wissen nicht, was ihnen blüht.

5

Erster Januar, gute Vorsätze

Ich beginne ein neues Notizbuch

für Fragen, die keine Antworten brauchen.

Wie lange hält sich der Schnee

auf den Zweigen des Vogelbeerstrauchs?

Gestern ging ich im Traum

auf einer Rolltreppe in die falsche Richtung,

ich wollte die Rückgabezentrale aufsuchen,

mein Verfallsdatum war abgelaufen.

Woher kommt meine unerträgliche Sanftmut?

Und, wie schon in den letzten Jahren,

warum hat der Stein nicht eine Stimme?

7

Die Wolken rasen, als liefe ein Ultimatum ab,

und die Zweige, in denen der Wind sich verirrt,

schlagen verzweifelt die Luft.

Aus den Schulen der Stille

mit ihren hochgebildeten Fenstern

fällt kaum noch Licht auf den Weg.

Wissen ist nicht mehr schön,

es ergreift uns nicht mehr.

Ach, ihr weitblickenden Wolken!

Irgendwo spielen noch Kinder,

man hört ihr begeistertes Rufen.
Und plötzlich trudelt ein Ball
mir vor die Füße, und ein Kind befiehlt:
Spiel mit!

8

Auf den verschlafenen Wegen ging ich
hinunter zum See, um der Post zu entkommen.
Seit Tagen redet der Briefträger mit mir
von den Letzten Dingen: dem Duft
der Weidenkätzchen nach dem Regen,
der Wahrheitstreue unserer Erinnerungen
und daß man um Himmels willen Gott
nicht immer wieder mit der Vernunft
quälen sollte. Unterm Redeschwall
streckt er mir Todesanzeigen zu,
schwarzrandige Briefe, mit Rilkes Versen
vom Hiersein bedruckt oder mit Benn.
Es ist vollbracht,
unsere Generation nimmt Abschied.
Welche Verse von uns werden es
in die Große Anthologie schaffen?
Der See lag vor mir wie schmelzendes Wachs,
ruhig und träge und ohne Tiefe,
wie ein kindlicher Traum des Glücks.

NIKOLASSE, FEBURAR 2015

Ich soll hier aufgewachsen sein,

zwischen unserer Kirche und dem Kleist-Grab,

zwei Gottesorte für unsere höheren Ziele.

Auf der Rehwiese weideten Schafe,

aber wie sollten wir mit dem Hirten sprechen,

der nur die Sprache der Lämmer verstand?

You are leaving the American Sector.

Keiner von uns wußte,

wie der Hase läuft und wohin.

Hier, an den warmen Sommertagen,

haben wir davon geträumt, der Welt

brüderlich in die Speichen zu greifen.

Über uns eine große und eine kleine Wolke,

Mutter und Kind, mehr brauchte nicht sein.

Das Grab meiner Eltern ist schon im Angebot,

so schnell hat sich das Rad gedreht.

BERLIN, STADT DER KINDHEIT

Am Ende der Straße, da
wo sie einen Knick macht,
damit man nicht sieht,
ob sie weitergeht,

steht ein alter Hund,
der offenbar nicht weiß,
wie er nach Hause kommt.
Mir geht es ähnlich.

Ich war mir ganz sicher,
daß ich hier einmal gelebt habe.
Im Haus gegenüber
wurde damals eine Bombe entschärft.

Eine junge Frau bringt triumphierend
ihren Müll zur Tonne,
als enthielte er ihr ganzes Leben.
Weg damit. Sie mustert mich lange,

kommt aber zu anderen Schlüssen.
Aus einem offenen Fenster
dringt das Weinen eines Kindes.
Es muß dieses Haus gewesen sein.

WIE ES NIE MEHR SEIN WIRD

Noch einmal will ich den Wiesenkümmel

riechen, in Essigwasser getaucht;

die geschuppten Wolken über Kayna sehen;

den Fliegen zuhören,

die ihre Totenlieder singen an der Fensterscheibe;

die Schatten beobachten, die ums Haus schleichen,

um das Buch des Lebens einzudunkeln;

das helle Licht spüren, die Augen Gottes.

Dort, wo ich kleinlaut war, wenn die Sonne unterging,

rot wie ein Hahnenkamm.

Was hast du gesagt? Nichts. Ich habe nur etwas

fallen lassen hinter den sieben Bergen, wo Europa

aufhörte und meine Kindheit begann.

MEINE GROßMUTTER

erwartete weder Lohn noch Strafe

vom Leben, sie wußte genau,

um was es nicht geht, der Rest war

für Männer in Uniform,

oder für Philosophen.

Handschuhe zum Beispiel zog sie

nie an, um sie nicht zu beschmutzen.

An ihrem Unterricht nahmen teil

Kamille, Kornblume und Saubohne,

alle bestanden mit Auszeichnung,

weil es gab keine Düngemittel

nach dem großen Krieg.

Was für prächtige Saubohnen!

Als ich heute hier in den Bergen,

die meine Großmutter nie gesehen hat,

das graue Gras vom Vorjahr betrachtete,

das endlich wieder aufblicken konnte

nach langer winterlicher Belagerung,

mußte ich daran denken,

daß sie vom Leben weder Lohn

noch Strafe erwartete.

Aber was dann? Nichts,

um die Wahrheit zu sagen, nichts.

GRUNEWALD

für Markus Barth

1

Der Frost, der den Vögeln die Stimme abwürgt;

und auch meine Worte, eben noch ein Schlüssel zur Welt,

sind plötzlich verstummt.

Eine Meise im Fenster, sie schaut mich an

wie ein tibetanischer Mönch. Piep, sage ich,

Gott hat es nicht gut gemeint mit euch Vögeln!

Ihr könnt üben und üben und bringt doch

keinen Gesang in die Welt.

2

Man kann mich besuchen, der A19 hält

direkt vor dem Haus. Alles, was ich mache,

wird sich gegen mich kehren.

Manchmal öffne ich nachts das Fenster und höre

der Dunkelheit zu. Es grenzt an Folter,

wenn die Stimmen ins Haus kommen

und man die Sprecher nicht sieht.

Bitte keine Reden am Grab, ein frommer Wunsch.

Und streut die Asche dem Flieder in die Augen,

bevor sich der Wind ihrer annimmt.

3

Im Flur meiner Wohnung hängt ein Spiegel, der weiß

mehr über mich als ich selbst. Ein Spezialist für Güte,

jeden Tag gehe ich ihm auf den Leim. Seine Orakel,

sein wehrloses Lächeln! Du sollst leben, murmelt er mir zu,

einfach leben, mehr verlange ich nicht. Und ich: Aber ich will

mich sehen, schrei ich ihn an, einmal im Leben will ich mich

gesehen haben, ist das zu viel verlangt? Sei still, sagt er sachlich,

in vier Wochen leben wir wieder getrennt.

WISSENSCHAFTSKOLLEG

für Luca Giuliani

Der kleine See gegenüber, der mich jeden Morgen begrü.t,
ist Teil eines größeren, durch dunkle Adern verbunden.
Wie ein Auge, in dem nachts die Träume schlafen,
wenn die Sprache sich von der Wissenschaft erholt.
Baden verboten. Liederliche Weiden bewachen das Ufer,
und Enten, den Kopf streng gesenkt wie Mönche,
bewegen das stehende Wasser.
Von den schläfrigen Villen mit ihren feuchten Kellern,
in denen die Schatten der Vorbesitzer an denWänden lehnen,
führen Treppen zum See. Manchmal sehe ich Menschen
dort stehen, mit angestrengtem Lächeln, als ahnten sie,
daß ihnen in Wahrheit nichts gehört.
Die Sonne scheint stolz zu sein auf diesen See,
nur die Vögel halten sich nicht an das Gebot der Stille.
Man will mehr vom Leben haben, als das Leben zu geben
bereit ist, lautet das Gesetz unsres Instituts.
Unser Chef ist Archäologe, er kann ein Lied davon singen.

WIKO 2

Ich muß jetzt gehn, die Putzkolonne

steht schon vor der Tür, damit dem neuen Gast

das Bett bezogen wird. Ich hinterlasse

eine leere Zukunft, zwei Dutzend Bücher,

die mich nicht halten konnten, einen Fön

und hundert Blätter im Papierkorb,

bedeckt mit Zeichen, mit denen ich

das Schweigen überlisten wollte.

Die Vögel, die mich morgens weckten,

werden bleiben, der schwarze Bach, der Zeuge

meines Scheiterns, der Wehmut ein Gedicht

zu widmen, der Ahorn, die Akazien, Staub.

Und auch das Leuchten lasse ich zurück, die Stille

und den Schatten in den leeren Räumen.

Das Leben, heißt es, wird vom Tod erwärmt.

Stimmt das? Der Kehraus kann beginnen.

RÄTSEL

Gartengeräte, leere Blumentöpfe, eine Sense ohne Halt

und ein namenloser Stein, den ich wer weiß wo

aufgelesen habe zu späterem Gebrauch.

Eine dämmrige Welt, trocken und still,

das stille Alphabet des Glücks.

Zwei Spiegelscherben auf dem Gartentisch:

die eine zeigt den, der ich nicht mehr bin,

die andre den, der ich nicht mehr werden kann.

Dazwischen hockt das Unglück mit den tausend Augen,

die alles sehn, auch das, was es nicht gibt

und niemals geben wird.

EUROPA

Ich bin immer noch ein blutiger Laie,

wenn es darum geht, die Welt des Guten

von der Welt des Bösen zu unterscheiden.

Es ist alles viel einfacher.

Als ich heute nach Hause ging,

sah ich die Kinder Europa spielen

mit all den schönen Sterbensworten,

die im Schwange sind.

Ein grauer Himmel, der nicht tröstete,

lag auf der Stadt, doch als ich

bei der Linde innehielt im Hof,

hörte ich den Chor der Wurzeln singen.

NEU-SCHNEE

Über Nacht der Schnee
auf den Bäumen. Die Höflichkeit,
mit der er die Zweige berührt,
danach die Bücher, das Auge,
das stotternde Herz.
Wie lange es braucht, die Kindheit zu verstehen,
denn auch der Schnee kennt die Scham.
Ich weiß nicht, wo ich suchen soll unterm Weiß,
und was ich finde, sind Steine, die rot werden,
wenn man sie höflich berührt.

MORSCHE BÄUME

Als die Schatten endlich versammelt waren
vor und in meinen Augen,
der Schatten der Eibe dem Schatten des Ahorns
sich ausgeliefert hatte und die armseligen Rosen,
fast nicht mehr sichtbar, sich ein anderes Herz
suchen mußten für die Nacht,
sah ich, wie ein Licht die Bäume umgab,
ein silbriger Schimmer wie bei morschem Holz.
Wenn die Linde sich nicht täuscht,
und das tut sie selten im Alter, wird in der Nacht
ein Sturm uns an der Gurgel packen, einer von denen,
die kein Mitleid haben mit morschen Bäumen.

DIE KIEFER UND DER BERGAHORN

Zu groß geraten ist die Kiefer,

die sich mit dem Ahorn messen muß

im Kampf ums Licht.

Keiner mag sie hier im Viertel,

wo man Blätter liebt, nicht Nadeln.

Gemeiner Efeu hat sie fest im Griff,

der wird ihr bald den Garaus machen,

hoffentlich.

Ich schaue diesem Baum seit Jahren zu,

wie er sich in den Himmel drängt,

und wie der Ahorn alles tut

sich günstig von ihm abzusetzen.

Ich kann mich nicht entscheiden,

ob ich einen lieber haben sollte,

beide nehmen mir die freie Sicht,

die ich in ihrer Jugend hatte.

Ich brauche Aussicht, Weite, Perspektive,

jetzt stehen grüne Wächter mir vor Augen,

die ihr Leben an dem meinen messen,

das, da sind sich beide sicher,

kürzer sein wird als das ihre.

KINDLICHE ÜBUNGEN

Nimm das Gras, das hilflose Gras
in die Hand, bevor du es schneidest.
Oder, als gnostische Übung, leg den Stein
zurück auf die Wunde, die er am Boden
hinterließ. Oder schau, mit denkendem Auge,
auf eine stille Wasserfläche, die dich nicht erkennt.
Oder, noch schwieriger, geh auf den Engel zu,
der sich unter der Tür nicht entscheiden kann,
ob er ins Haus gehört oder ins Freie.
Oder horch, ganz einfach, auf das Geräusch
der Schritte auf gefrorenem Schnee.
Oder denk dir eine Welt ohne dich und ohne
die andern – betrachte, mit anderen Worten,
mit dem Staunen eines Kindes die Schattenseite
der Welt, um, vor aller Versöhnung, dem Trost
nicht in die Arme zu laufen.

DER NUSSBAUM, DIE ZEIT

Der Nußbaum mußte dran glauben,
um die Sehnsucht nach Ordnung zu stillen.
Vor zehn Jahren habe ich einen Trieb
in die Erde gesteckt, einen puritanischen Stecken,
nach drei Jahren die ersten Nüsse,

rätselhafte Früchte, angeblich

Abbilder unseres Gehirns.

Alles wird der Ordnung geopfert,

die Kindheit, die Jugend, der Garten, die Sorge.

Nur mein Gehirn ist so unordentlich geblieben

wie der ungehobelte Nußbaum,

der dem Hasel das Wasser abgräbt.

Aber ich brauchte seinen Schatten,

um mich auszuruhen und zu schauen,

meinetwegen auf Kosten der Wahrheit.

Den freien Platz besetzt jetzt das Unglück,

in dessen Schatten sich die Zeit niederläßt,

die gefräßige Zeit, die alles an sich reißt,

über und unter der Erde, am hellichten Tag.

DAS GRAB

Schau, der leuchtende Saum

unserer Fußspuren, die zum Grab führen,

als hätte der Mond sich geteilt

und schiene, bitter und kalt und stark,

nur auf unseren Weg und wollte schon

nichts mehr wissen vom Leben

in unseren Körpern.

Laß uns nebeneinanderliegen.

Mein Hunger gehört schon den Wurzeln,

mein Durst den Steinen,

meine Wörter den winzigen Tieren,

die uns das Bett bereiten für kurze Zeit.

EINE ANDERE GESCHICHTSSCHREIBUNG

Windstille. Ein Hund schnüffelt vorbei,

ohne mich eines Blickes zu würdigen.

Er hinterläßt eine genaue Wegbeschreibung

im Schnee. Die Vögel lesen ernsthaft

in den Bucheckern, die schwarz auf dem Weiß

liegen: Mach es dir nicht zu leicht.

In der Ferne der klagende Ruf einer Sirene,

ein Ton, mit dem man Schlangen beschwört.

Als reichte die Stille nicht aus,

ein anderes Leben zu denken.

ALLTAG

Wenn ich morgens die Zeitung hole,

kommt mir das eigene Leben vor

wie die flüchtige Skizze eines anderen,

das im Vermischten haust.

Die Zeitung ist schwer,

als hätte das Böse Gewicht.
Die Geschichte frißt sich auf,
bald ist nichts mehr übrig
außer den Schlagzeilen.
Es wird immer sinnloser,
an einen Sinn zu glauben,
der schwerer wiegt als das Vermischte.
Wenn der Apfelbaum nicht wär
in meinem Garten, ich gäbe auf.

8. MAI 2013

Wenn mich nicht alles täuscht,
hat Gott sich in meinem Apfelbaum versteckt.
Zum ersten Mal seit Jahren hat er sich
ausgerechnet diesen Baum ausgesucht,
nicht gerade einen aufrechten Vertreter
seiner Gattung, dessen Früchte holzig sind
und bitter schmecken. Aber die Bienen
lieben ihn. Wenn ich mich, barfuß,
an seinen Stamm lehne, höre ich
ihren Erzählungen zu, von einem
Meer aus Honig ist die summende Rede,
das auch Moses nicht teilen kann.
Ich kann Gott lachen hören.
Da halten selbst die Vögel den Schnabel.

AUF DEM LAND

Wer sagt denn, der Himmel

sei leer, und weltarm sei einer,

der sich unter ihm krümmt

unter Aufsicht der Sterne?

Auf der Türschwelle, daheim,

liegt der Totenpaß,

den die Katze gebracht hat.

Jetzt nimm einen Zweig

vom Holunder, die Dämonen

in die Flucht zu schlagen,

die unter dem Türstock hocken,

als würden sie auf dich warten.

MÄRZ 2014, UNTERM APFELBAUM

Dies ist die Stunde der Allesversteher,

die mit gesundem Menschenverstand

in der Asche wühlen nach Beweisen,

die sie selbst verbrannt haben.

Enttäuschte Pädagogen.

Aber die Asche nimmt der Wind mit,

der Allesfresser, der sie übers ganze Land

ausstreut, über Gläubige und Ungläubige,

über die verstummenden Bienenstöcke

und über unsere verstörten Herzen,

die taktlos ins Leere schlagen.

Die alte Kunst, Widersprüche auszuhalten,

um das Unverständliche der Schönheit

zu erfahren, ist vergessen wie manches Handwerk

oder überflüssig wie das Recht auf Wunder.

Ich sitze müßig unterm Apfelbaum,

lausche dem Selbstgespräch der Zweige

und sehe den heiligen Schatten zu,

wie sie sich aufs Sterben vorbereiten,

lange vor Sonnenuntergang.

2015

Es sollte sein das Jahr der dicken Hummeln,

das Jahr des Futterals, der hohen Zeit,

der Wärme, die aus Frost und Nebel steigt,

das Jahr der weiten Himmel und der klugen Bücher,

die im Schatten von der Zukunft träumen,

das Jahr der Bienen und des Honigs.

Es sollte sein ein langes Jahr der Spinne,

die ihren Faden enger knüpft an meinem Hals,

das Jahr der armen Worte und des Mundes,

der sie wärmt. Es sollte sein: ein Jahr.

HERBST 2015

Mit bloßen Füßen
streicht die Nacht durchs Gras
und färbt die Äpfel schwarz.

Aus großen Kübeln
hat der Herbst seine Schwermut
in den Garten geschüttet,
und nichts davon will
im Erdreich versinken.

Flüchtlinge, leere Rucksäcke
über der Schulter,
tragen die Kälte durchs Land.
Einer zeigt eine Fotografie herum
von der Sonne überm Meer.
Seit er an Land ist,
läßt sie sich nicht mehr blicken.

SPAZIERGANG IM MAI, 2016

Der Himmel eine graue Schale voller Asche,
in der sich ein unersättlicher Wind vergräbt.
Die Erde dampft von früher Wärme und lockt
die Wurzeln ans Licht. Ich will kein Kind mehr sein,

will das Gras nicht mehr um Rat fragen,

wenn die Steine in sich gekehrt schweigen,

als ginge es tatsächlich um Leben und Tod.

Es geht um etwas anderes, das sich nicht sagen läßt

in meiner Sprache. Die Toten wissen es,

die Nacht für Nacht in meinem Kopf sich streiten,

bis ihnen der Morgen die Stimme abdreht.

Hier und da noch weiße Flecken, Schnee,

der sich nicht lösen läßt, und am Stauwehr

die gesammelten Werke der alten Blätter.

Wenn nur das wütende Schluchzen des Windes

nicht wäre, träte die Wahrheit vielleicht ans Licht,

die naive Wahrheit, die dem Gras so ähnlich sieht.

LE MONDE, JANUAR 2017

für Yasmina Reza

Ein leichter trauriger Morgen

nach einer erbärmlichen langen Nacht.

Mit Honig in den Adern gehe ich ums Haus

wie eine Katze, der Wind lehnt am Tor,

und der Ahorn gibt sich alle Mühe,

mit seinen spitzen Schatten das Gras zu kitzeln.

Wem man dienen soll? Der Wahrheit

und dem Volk. Aber man ist nie der, der man ist,

trotz aller Arbeit kommt ein anderer vorbei

als der, den man erwartet hat. Er ist schon

im Haus, ein Prediger der Gleichgültigkeit,

und hält Reden wie auf dem Markt, Eis

klirrt in seinen Worten. Hell wird es

nicht mehr werden, weil wir den Schalter

nicht finden, der umgelegt werden muß,

bevor wir umgelegt werden.

Der kleine Mensch von nebenan

mit seinem Lichtlein, das als Blitz gedacht war,

in dem die Welt zu lesen wäre

wie ein Buch.

IM ENGLISCHEN GARTEN, JANUAR 2017

Über dem Schnee eine bedrohliche Lichtflut

wie ein lang anhaltender Schrei,

der huscht über die nicht mehr erkennbare Welt,

als drängte ein Fieber zum Ausbruch.

Wenn man vom Wehr aus auf den Fluß blickt,

sehen in der Tiefe die Steine aus wie ein Setzkasten

der Erinnerung, den ein Schwarm Elritzen

blitzschnell verwirrt zu einer neuen Sprache.

Wie oft habe ich hier gestanden,

auf der Selbstm.rderbrücke, das brummende Mahlen

der Stadt im Rücken, und auf das Wasser gestarrt,

das mir wie die Zeit selber vorkam.

Unverhofft gaben die Krähen den Segen.

IM WINTER

Bei der Schneewehe lag ich,
bei den Lärchen, wo im Herbst
der Wind die Schafe sammelt,
und wartete auf das Ende
der Zerstreuung. Kein Vogel mehr
in den Ebereschen, kein Laut,
kein Durcheinander im weißen Staat.
Unergründlich und leer.
Ich sah, bei geschlossenen Augen,
die rissigen Hände meiner Großmutter,
wie sie den Apfel viertelte
mit sicherer Hand
und uns zu Gleichen machte
an einem Nachmittag im Winter.

ZUR LAGE

Man hat uns bestohlen,
aber wir wissen nicht,
was uns fehlt.
Nach Hause gekommen,
fühlen wir uns erleichtert.
Der Dieb, den wir kennen,
hütet sein Geheimnis,
er will uns schonen.

II

»Der Begriff des Reisens
ist mit dem Ankommen
verbunden. Aber will
man überhaupt ankommen?«

Günter Metken

EINMAL EINFACH

Es ist schön, mit dem Zug
durch Deutschland zu fahren,
immer zu spät.
Du hast es nicht eilig.
Schrebergärten kriechen
um die Städte herum
wie Schnecken.
Am Ende des Lebens
wird dir ein Tag geschenkt,
den darfst du verprassen
am Bahnhofsbuffet
zusammen mit Tauben und Spatzen.

HERBS AM BODENSEE

November. Noch steht der Mais
wie eine starre braune Mauer
und nimmt mein Flüstern auf.
Kein lautes Wort, kein Schrei,
nur leises Zweifeln, ob die Kutte hält
über den hellgelben Körnern.
Radikal ungläubig, ist es das,
was uns eint oder trennt?
Der Mais spricht alle Sprachen.

Über der Reichenau, wo die Schrift
in die Welt kam, kreist ein Milan,
und die Bücher, die immer recht
haben wollen, weil es sie sonst
nicht gäbe und der Tod tatenlos
zusehen mü.te, wie wir im Mais
verschwinden, halten dicht.

HOTELZIMMER IN HANOVER

Das Zimmer ist leer.
Die Tauben auf dem Fensterbrett
sprechen Russisch für Anfänger,
bevor sie vergiftet werden.
Ein Bett wird hereingeschoben,
es leuchtet im Dunkel;
dann ein Stuhl, Wasser, Bleistifte,
die sich an Romane erinnern.
Eine Lampe macht keinen Sinn.
Die Exportweltmeister schlafen,
do not disturb. Der letzte Schrei.
Eine Reisegruppe aus China
irrt durch die Heizung,
sie möchte ins Internet.
Auf einer Bank vor dem Hotel
wird eine Pipeline angezapft,

russisches Öl, eine konspirative Erpressung.
Gegenüber der Bahnhof,
um 5 Uhr 12 gelingt die Flucht
mit allen ungeschriebenen Büchern.

NÄCHTLICHE SZENE

Der Bahnhof ist schon abgefahren;
nur die Gleise erinnern noch
an den Handel mit Menschen.
Den Körper mit Salz eingerieben,
ein Ziegenfell über der Schulter,
suchen wir zwischen den Gleisen
das Weite, das ins Land gegangen ist –
nicht aus Barmherzigkeit,
sondern aus Pflicht. Alle Uhren
sind bis an die Zähne bewaffnet
und hinken der Zeit hinterher.

ZBIGNIEW HERBERTS STUHL

An einem Tag im März 2014 in Warschau
darf ich auf Zbigniews Stuhl sitzen.
Die Sonne scheint durch die kahlen Äste
der mürrischen Bäume vor seinem Fenster

und läßt den Staub nicht zur Ruhe kommen
über den Büchern, eine solide Wand
aus Philosophie und Kunstgeschichte
in fünf Sprachen. Hat er die Katze noch gekannt,
die vor den griechischen Klassikern liegt?
Mit seiner Spinnenschrift hat er die Bücher
vollgekritzelt: Alles war anders,
als gesagt wird, sagt seine zittrige Schrift,
die den krummen Pfaden der Geschichte folgt
bis ins helle Herz der Schönheit.
Und dann betritt Herr Cogito das Zimmer,
die keuchende Stimme voller Rauch,
setzt sich mir gegenüber auf einen neuen Stuhl
und spricht vom Verschwinden der Religion
in der Theologie. Wir brauchen ein Leben,
sagt er, um zu begreifen, was ein Fremder
mit einem Blick erkennt, daß wir nämlich
so unbedeutend sind wie alle anderen auch.
Herr Cogito lächelt. Es wird schnell dunkel.
Warschau ist bald wieder eine dunkle Stadt.

WEGRAND

Geh du deinen Weg,
den holprigen,
ich warte hier,
wo Minze und Geißblatt
das Kreuz überwuchern.
Ich habe ein offenes Herz,
durch das die Ameisen laufen,
ich kann ihre Beine spüren.
Sie tragen mir das Herz ab
mit schöner Geschäftigkeit.
Das große Kunstwerk Wiese,
in Farbe, und das Kreuz,
das nicht zu sehen ist
mit bloßem Auge.
Wenn du zurückkommst,
wirst du mich nicht mehr finden,
aber das Kreuz wird dir sagen,
wo ich war.

CLUJ/BELVEDERE

Noch hält der Nebel die Kirchen versteckt,
doch ich höre ihr römisch-katholisches Murmeln.
Auch ich halte mich bereit.
Die Ambulanz fährt die Toten der Nacht
sicher nach Hause ins Land jenseits der Wälder.
Wenn der Schatten der Tauben die Hunde streift,
gehen die Lichter aus, und die Welt wird verständlicher.
In der anbrechenden Helle sehe ich
auch die geschwätzige Mafia der Spatzen.

VOR WIEN UND IN WIEN

Gutmütige Wolken, wie Bauern, die auf dem Markt
ihr Gemüse verkaufen, begleiten uns bis ins Zentrum.
Die Stadt denkt nicht daran, mein Leben zu retten.
Im Hotelzimmer steht eine Mauer aus Worten,
die ich im Halbschlaf übersetze.
Ich weiß nicht, auf welcher Seite du liegst,
aber ich höre dich atmen.
Wenn ich ein Streichholz entzünde,
springt das Dunkel ins Zimmer:
Wir dürfen nicht gesehen werden in Wien.

IM SÜDEN, AM MEER

Ginster und andere Stechpflanzen, dieselbe Schule,
genügsame Begleiter, die wochenlang ohne Wasser auskommen,
aber immer tipptopp im Wind, von Insekten umschwärmt,
die wie an Schnüren gezogen auf- und absteigen
über der grünen Skulptur. Wie das Paradies aussieht?
Die Welt ist so angefüllt mit Elend, daß der Gesang
erfunden werden mußte, auch wenn er keine Lösung ist.
Es gibt keine Lösung, auch das Schreiben ist keine.
Manchmal schlägt eine Welle über die Klippe
und hinterläßt für Sekunden ein kleines Meer
auf dem Weg und den seltsamen Geruch nach Wasser
und heißem Staub. Der Horizont dunkelt ein
und gibt das Unmögliche preis, das sich dem Wort
widersetzt, dem untreuen Gehilfen. Jetzt ist es Zeit
für die Ameisen und ihre wimmelnde Schönfärberei.

TRAUM VOM 27. SEPTEMBER, MODENA

In einem knallbunten Prospekt,
der im Hotel auslag,
wurde die Stadt beschrieben,
in die ich verbracht worden war.
Einen Namen hatte sie nicht.
In glühenden Fußnoten
war von Eseln die Rede,

deren Schreie gesammelt werden

gegen Fieber und Durchfall.

Die Rechnung, wie immer, ohne den Wirt.

OPFERN

Im Dom von Modena, einem strahlenden Tempel

der Andacht, auf dem die Vögel sich wohl fühlen,

was die hellen Steine zu Tränen rührt.

Jeder dunklen Hand gab ich ein Geldstück,

den Rest warf ich klirrend in einen Opferstock,

der sich lateinisch bedankte. Bleib stehen,

rief ein Greis einem Kind hinterher; ich blieb.

Ich war froh, mich nicht schämen zu müssen.

Nach der Messe, im offenen Mittag, stand ich

lange vor den Fotos der Opfer des Widerstands,

die an der Nordwand angeschlagen sind

mit ihren Namen und den Daten ihres kurzen Besuchs

auf der Erde. Manche hatten noch ihre Zigarette

im Mundwinkel hängen, alle schauten mich an.

Eine Wand aus Blicken, die mich begleiteten

bis zu meinem Hotel, Libertá, Best Western,

gleich hinter der Synagoge, wo Soldaten die Klage

bewachen, wie überall in Europa. Wir müssen Gott

zurück in die Schule schicken, dachte ich. Eine Spinne

arbeitete in einer Ecke des winzigen Zimmers

unerbittlich an ihrem Faden, es ist hohe Zeit.

3. OKTOBER 2015

Am Tag der Deutschen Einheit
saß ich mit Maimonides in Córdoba
in einem Café hinter der Synagoge.
Er sprach mit Würde und Grazie
über Toleranz, kaum zu verstehen
zwischen den schwatzenden Touristen.
Ich wartete auf einen Anruf.
Vor uns lag ein Hund und hechelte
nach einem Namen. Du, lieber Hund,
gehörst zu einem schriftlosen Volk,
das gegen Hunger und Unwissenheit kämpft.
Alle Gäste im Café telefonierten,
als wollten sie mehr voneinander wissen.
Maimonides schwieg.
Allmählich verlor sich das Leben, doch so langsam,
daß Hoffnung aufkam, es könnte sich
eine Zukunft vorstellen vor dem Tod.

HOTEL VILLA POLITI, SYRAKUS

Vor dem Zimmer 130 der Eingang
in die Unterwelt, winzige Vögel
bewachen die Pforte,
die selber unsichtbar bleibt.

Es ist so dunkel,

daß man sich leicht als den begreift,

der man ist.

Um Mitternacht stehen Fremdenführer bereit,

die einen durch den Honig der Erinnerung

begleiten, ein zähes Geschäft.

Dann hört man die Toten tuscheln,

besessen von der Frage,

warum die Lebenden am Leben bleiben wollen.

Am Ende des Ganges ein schwaches Licht,

dort wird die heilige Lucia begraben.

Auch sie hat nur mit Zitronen gehandelt,

wie wir alle, denen die Worte fehlen

für einen Pakt mit dem Teufel.

TIEFFLUG

Wie ein Friedhof sieht der Flughafen aus;

bis zum Abend finden noch dreißig Beerdigungen statt,

in Toulouse z. B., in Abu Dhabi und in Berlin, und die Schlange

der Menschen, die nach Belgrad oder Izmir wollen, ist lang.

Erinnerst du dich an den Friedhof von Izmir,

wo es das beste Pistazieneis gab, das beste der Welt,

und uns die Lebenden wie verkannte Tote vorkamen,

die vergessen hatten, in welcher Sprache

sie mit uns reden sollten? Ein letzter Aufruf für Herrn Hatake, der an seinem Grab in Paris erwartet wird, aber

sich bei Münster angestellt hat, zur Urnenbestattung.

Mit jedem Ticket erhält man eine kleine Sanduhr

aus Plastik, die im Morgengrauen abgelaufen ist,

manche halten sie schräg, um die Zeit zu betrügen.

Furchtbare Musik aus allen Lautsprechern!

Und wo früher das Wiener Kaffeehaus war,

darf man jetzt, gemeinsam mit den Toten, beten.

Meine Nachbarin in der Schlange, aus Warschau,

hat ein dickes Buch über die Gottesanbeterin geschrieben,

die dazu verdammt ist, ihr Männchen zu verzehren,

obwohl es nach nichts schmeckt.

SCHÖNHEIT

Im Zug heute, von Krefeld nach Köln,

ging eine Alte von Bank zu Bank

und bot Schönheit an.

Alles schaute zum Fenster hinaus,

um sie nicht anschauen zu müssen.

Sie hatte schwere, müde Hände,

an jedem Finger trug sie einen Ring.

Hände, die an die Ewigkeit glaubten.

Ihre Geschichte ist eine Erzählung,

die jeder kennt, auch wenn sie keiner versteht.

Was ist, wenn man die Gabe verweigert?

Ein Schulterzucken ging durchs Abteil.

Und die Alte, die Schönheit in Händen,

schlurfte weiter, durch den Zug hindurch

und dann hinaus, weil es

keine Türen gab im letzten Waggon.

Der Zug hielt an, wir mußten warten,

bis auf dem Gegengleis der Tod vorbeifuhr,

der sich verspätet hatte. Sechs Minuten.

Aber bis Köln, sagte der Lautsprecher,

holen wir das spielend wieder ein.

Gute Fahrt!

PESCARA, IM NOVEMBER

Das Meer spült Briefe an Land,

frankiert mit Schnee, geheime

Nachrichten für die Zeit

nach dem Tod.

In den Palmen wütet der Wind.

Mein kleiner Bleistift hält

zu mir, der Rest macht sich auf

ins Einfache, das unabhängig

sein will von aller Beschreibung.

OSTERSPAZIERGANG

Der Weg zurück über dem Meer, am Ginster entlang,
der den Schafen die Wolle stiehlt.
Ein Schiff zieht den Sonnenuntergang
übers Wasser wie in alten Legenden.
Der Strandhafer, erregt, als stünde etwas bevor,
und die Echsen sollen es verkünden.
Im Ginster wohnen die Götter, sie haben Hunger.
Ich bin der Führer der Unschlüssigen,
aber ich darf mich nicht umdrehen.
Vor mir der uralte Ölbaum, der Richter,
mit seinen tausend salzigen Augen,
er hat den Weg im Blick, der das Meer teilt.
Ein Gott ohne Füße, dachte ich,
der nicht weglaufen kann wie ich,
muß das Elend lange betrachten,
und erst wenn die Sonne verzischt ist,
kann er mein Begleiter werden
auf dem langen Weg nach Haus.

HOTEL KANET

Am Fenster meines Hotels Kanet in Skopje
flog plötzlich der Kohlweißling vorbei,
den ich von zu Hause kannte. Ich wollte nicht

glauben, daß er mir gefolgt war,

den langen staubigen Weg bis hierher,

aber seine Technik verriet ihn,

das nervöse Geflatter und der plötzliche Stillstand,

wenn er auf den Köpfen der Generäle ausruhte,

die eisern die Straßen säumen,

als gäbe es mehr zu beherrschen

als das braune Laub der Kastanien,

das schon im Juni den Herbst ahnen läßt.

Wie eine Marionette tanzte er vor meinem Fenster

und erzählte die Geschichte seiner Reise:

Die Polizei in Innsbruck hatte ihn durchgewunken,

die Serben, Kroaten und Albaner seine Flügel gestempelt,

ein kyrillisches Visum auf seiner weißen Seide.

Ich saß stumm auf dem Bett und sah ihm zu,

die Hitze machte uns beiden zu schaffen

und der Lärm eines Rock-Konzerts im Park.

Seine weiße taumelnde Schrift war leicht zu lesen

in der schwindenden Helle.

Mit letzter Kraft erreicht er die Zypressen,

die wie Kyrill und Method das Hotel bewachen.

Noch eine Stunde, dann wird er ein weißer Fleck sein

im Mulch unter den Bäumen, und die Mäuse werden sich

seiner Seele erbarmen. Ach, lieber Kohlweißling,

wie könnte ich je dich vergessen.

IN SKOPJE, 2015

Nacht, Zeit des Herzstillstands,
das Zimmer nebenan bleibt leer.
Ich bin der einzige Gast und horche
auf das ottomanische Geraune
der Maulbeerbäume.
Bin ich jetzt alt?
Die faltigen Arme, die zerfressene Hüfte
und überall Flecken auf der Haut,
sie ergeben ein Suchspiel:
Wenn du die Punkte richtig verbindest,
winkt dir als Hauptpreis ein Tod.
Vor dem Fenster wird ein Streichholz
gezündelt: Wird es die Welt erleuchten,
oder geht sie in Flammen auf?
Am Morgen zieht ein Gespräch ein
ins Zimmer nebenan, es wird geflüstert.
Verstanden habe ich nichts.

IN MAZEDONIEN

In Mazedonien geht man abends
verkehrt herum ins Lokal,
damit man nicht sieht,
wie man empfangen wird.
Die Linden folgen einem

über die Schwelle, sogar die Bienen

haben Zutritt zum Schankraum.

An den Tischen sitzen Bücher,

die einander auswendig kennen.

Hinter der Bar hängt ein Spiegel,

der Alexander den Großen zeigt,

wie er gerade vom Pferd fällt.

Nimm Wasser zum Anis-Schnaps,

das löst den Honig im Herzen

vor dem Infarkt.

IN DEN ABRUZZEN

Aus der Vogelperspektive,

die ich liebe, ist der Dorn

nicht zu sehen, die Calle Pineto,

wo das Massaker stattfand

vor siebzig Jahren. Schwarze Falter,

die im Licht des Feuers

zum Vorschein kommen, befreit

von Trägheit und Geschichte.

Was wir sagen, haben die Toten gespürt,

was wir wissen, wissen wir von ihnen.

Wir müssen,

wie verlorene Kinder, die Worte wiederholen,

damit wir am Leben bleiben,

die Calle Pineto läßt uns keine Wahl.

IN CASO DI EMERGENZA

für Anwar M. Shaikh

darf man den Aufzug nicht benutzen.
Aber auf der Treppe fehlen Stufen,
und auf denen, die noch halten,
kauern Familien und erzählen Anekdoten
über die Schönheit der Wolken.
Ein seltsames Hotel, ohne Dach
und ohne den Makel der Vollkommenheit.
Der Sturm drängt auf sachliche Klärung.
Aber wie immer, wenn man hier absteigt,
reißt plötzlich der Himmel auf
und zeigt, auf einer verblichenen Lichtung,
die Eröffnung des Konzils der Schwalben.

BERGRÜßUNG DES FREUNDES

Aus einer langen Abwesenheit
kehrst du zurück
zu uns verarmten Verwandten.
Wir erkennen dich an der
geschickten Bewegung der Hände,
mit der du die Gabel hältst
und das schartige Messer.
Wenn du die Dinge anschaust,

145

blühen sie auf, wie immer.

Dein Projekt in der Fremde,

die Verschlüsselung der Welt,

ist nicht abgeschlossen, auch wenn

du redest, als sei die Zukunft verbraucht.

Wir werden kleiner und kleiner,

wenn du vom großen Sagen sprichst,

den Kopf an die Mauer gelehnt

wie einer, der nicht von hier ist

und schon gar nicht von dort.

SCHAF

für Caspar von Lovenberg

Gestern dachte ich wieder an die Schafherde

in Mezin. Ich war aus dem Auto ausgestiegen,

schaute über die sanften Hügel der Gascogne,

die wirklich einladend sanft sind, und dachte,

mehr kann das Leben nicht bieten

als diese Wellen aus Weizen, Gerste und Sonnenblumen,

die einmal zum Meer wollten bei der Erschaffung der Welt.

Nicht jeder schafft es bis zum Meer.

Plötzlich, die Sonne im Mittag und ich ohne Schatten,

war ich von einer Schafherde umgeben.

Sie wollen dich erdrücken mit ihrer wolligen Nähe,

ging es mir durch den Kopf, und eine Schafsangst

kroch mir in sanften Wellen über den Leib.

Aber sie nahmen mich auf, sie behüteten mich,

ich wurde zum Schaf und bin es geblieben.

Andere wollen Hund sein mit Ohren, die fliegen,

wieder andere eine Katze und nichts als das.

Aber ich bin Schaf, ein Schaf unter Schafen,

ein angesehenes Mitglied der Herde.

NACH DEM FEST

Die Zelte waren abgebrochen,

jetzt waren wir die Überbleibsel.

Eine leere Festwiese am frühen Morgen,

bewacht von Linden mit der Seele von Hirten.

Die Steine wurden langsam wieder kalt.

Können Sie sich ausweisen?

Gebt acht, warnten die Worte,

bevor des Schnitters Sichel

sie zum Schweigen brachte.

Was nie wirklich wirklich war,

kann man nicht entschlüsseln.

AM WASSER

Lange und still
am Wasser eines Baches sitzen.
Alle vernünftigen Argumente
schwimmen vorbei, nichts hält auf,
das Wasser läßt sich nicht erweichen.
Geruch von Kiefernnadeln
und jungen Brennesseln, erhitzt.
Ein Blatt Sauerampfer im Mund,
der das Lachen verbietet.
Das größte Unglück bleibt,
daß wir den Mund nicht halten.
Alles, was man nicht gewesen ist.
Ein glitzernder Eilzug,
der nie Verspätung hat,
wenn man ihn fahren läßt.
Bleib sitzen, schweig,
leih dir keine Worte vom Wasser,
laß sie ziehen.
Halte dich an die Steine,
wenn dir nach Reden zumute ist.

SONNENBLUMENKERNE

für Ryszard Krynicki

Manchmal frage ich mich,
ob wir uns wiedersehen, die Madonna
mit dem Hermelin in Krakau z. B.
oder die Sonnenblumen in Laroche,
wenn sie die ausgetrockneten Köpfe
hängen lassen vor der Ernte
und keine Kraft mehr haben,
sich nach dem Licht zu richten.
Die Madonna, schreibt mir Ryszard,
zeigt noch immer ihr bekümmertes Gesicht.
Ich habe sie anders in Erinnerung,
heiter, wie eine Sonnenblume am Mittag.
So erinnere ich mir ein anderes Leben,
eine andere Vergangenheit,
die lange vor der Ernte beginnt.
Die Kerne der Sonnenblumen
aus Laroche kann ich kaufen,
drei Euro das Tütchen.
Die Schale muß man knacken,
den Rest spuckt man aus.

FLUG

Der Himmel ist voller Kondensstreifen,

als hätte man Götter gejagt.

Sie gehen geräuschlos über Leichen

und zerfallen, ohne Anfang und Ende.

Eine ohrenbetäubende Stille,

in der Drohnen sich wohl fühlen,

beladen mit christlichen Werten.

Im Flugzeug um mich herum

Feinde, die einmal Freunde waren.

Sie beherrschen die Kunst,

das Elend vergessen zu machen.

Die Drohnen fliegen dem Tod voraus,

damit er auf keinen Widerstand trifft,

bevor wir landen im Jetzt

und verglühn.

III

»Die transzendentale Seite
der Kunst ist immer eine Form
des Gebets.«

John Berger

VORBILDER

Bitte, nehmt euch ein Beispiel
an den Bienen. Jede einzelne Wabe
wird gleichmäßig gefüllt, auch im Winter
ist genug da für alle. Hört ihr,
wie sie trotzdem das Lob
der Unvollkommenheit summen? Unsere Welt,
ob mit oder ohne Königin,
ist im Sprechen entstanden, jedes Wort
zungengeboren, aus dem Mund
entlassen ins Geläufige. Die Bienen
übersetzen, und der Wind, der ums Haus
geht wie ein Dieb, sammelt ein
und macht einen Vers draus,
den wir nur nachsprechen müssen.

IM PARK DER MUSIK

für Alfred Brendel, von Herzen

Das Tor steht immer offen, jeder kann eintreten
und auf dem Kies ein Geräusch hinterlassen,
auch Terror und Krieg sind herzlich eingeladen.
Wer ein Messer bei sich hat oder eine Pistole,
tritt gegen Amseln an, Spatzen und Tauben,
die den Flugzeugen nachfliegen, wenn es kracht.

Auch die Kinder lieben es laut, wenn sie

den Schall fangen wollen mit offenen Händen.

Und dann wird es plötzlich so still,

daß man die Klagen der Fliegen hören kann

und wie mein Buch lautlos die Sprache wechselt.

In der hintersten Ecke des Parks, wo,

gegen die ehernen Statuten der Zeit,

das Dunkel sich eingenistet hat wie altes Gras,

dreht Schubert das knarrende Rad der Sehnsucht,

als gäbe es noch eine Welt, die ihn braucht.

DAS BUCH DER BLÄTTER

Die Sonne, die jetzt den oberen Teil

des Ahorns aufleuchten läßt und im Buch

der Blätter, das keinen Anfang kennt und kein Ende,

eine Seite liest, mahnt zur Eile.

In jedem Blatt ist das Zentrum anwesend,

noch im letzten, das schon im Dunkel hängt.

Der Wind liest mit, er überspringt die Seite,

wenn der Specht auf einem Punkt besteht

und die Finken die Zeilen vertauschen,

damit das Volkslied sich nicht singen läßt

in alter Manier.

DAS SCHÖNE HAUS

für Wolfgang Rihm

Nichts gehört dir in diesem Haus,

das steht über der Tür in gotischer Schrift,

beleckt von Efeu und Wicken, von Bienen

geliebt und auch von Mücken.

Der Schlüssel ist auf Reisen

an diesem schönen Tag,

er schläft in anderen Schlössern.

Der Ahorn, ein alter Meister,

übergibt seine Geschenke dem Wind,

und der Geruch von Flieder hält sich

in der Hecke, aneinandergepreßt steht sie da

wie eine Anthologie von Liebesgedichten,

die keiner mehr lesen will.

Hier soll der freie Wille leben,

wenn er nicht von Haus zu Haus geht

und sich verkauft zu Schleuderpreisen,

behauptet der Nachbar, eingehüllt

in seinen Mantel aus Stein.

Wenn du das Ohr an die Tür preßt,

hörst du eine Uhr ticken, so laut,

als wollte sie die Zeit aufwecken,

damit der Tod wieder zu tun hat,

der faul unter dem Apfelbaum liegt

und sein Herz von Disteln befreit,

denn bald soll wieder Winter sein.

ANDACHT

Unter der Autobahnbrücke
wird eine Kirche gebaut
aus Abfall, als Altar dient
ein alter Kinderwagen.
Worte der Vergebung und
Gnade. Erinnerungen,
die keiner mehr braucht.
Der Pfarrer ist uralt
und meistens betrunken.
Aber er hat sich in Gott
verbissen, und jeder
hört ihm andächtig zu,
wenn er die Welt verflucht.

RHETORIK

Nach Sonnenuntergang, hieß es,
hält Demosthenes einen Vortrag
im Steinbruch vor der Stadt.
Wir waren da, auch die,
die nur Bahnhof verstehen,
wenn es um Wahrheit geht.

Er klaubte Kieselsteine auf,
die er sich in den Mund steckte,

um die Zunge geschmeidig zu machen.

Wenn er Kummer sagte oder Klage,

hüpfte ihm ein Stein

von den Lippen.

Am Ende, mit leerem Mund,

nahm er ein schnell wirkendes Gift.

Die Zuhörer, schläfrig und verdrossen,

machten sich auf den Heimweg.

Ich sammelte, als letzter, die Tränen auf,

bevor sie trockneten.

RASTSCHLAG FÜR DICHTERLESUNGEN

Man muß leise sprechen,

immer leiser,

um nicht von allen gehört zu werden.

Die Lippen aufeinanderpressen,

damit die Wahrheit sich schwertut.

Auf das Atmen der Stadt hören.

Und niemals aufblicken,

um das Unglück nicht sehen zu müssen.

Jede Erklärung des Unglücks

bedeutet eine Vermehrung des Jammers.

Das innere Rätsel braucht wenige Worte,

man kann es noch kürzer sagen.

SCHATTENWIRTSCHAFT

Wie Galgen sehen die Bäume aus,

ihrer Blätter entledigt nach dem Gewitter.

Unterm Baum hocken Menschen,

die vergraben ihre Pässe,

wie seit Menschengedenken.

Schuhe, auf einen Haufen geworfen,

wer braucht noch Schuhe?

Die Zeiger der Uhr nehmen sich Zeit,

die Zeit, die ich brauche,

dem Bild zu entkommen.

SCHNEE

Ich habe den weißen Mantel berührt

und unter dem Mantel zwei warme Länder,

Arm und Reich, in meiner erfrorenen Hand.

Ist die Erzählung zu Ende?

Unter dem Schnee wartet das Eis,

das bringt dich zerbrochen ins Tal.

ÜBER THRONE AND STÜHLE

War es nicht gestern,
daß wir noch alle auf dem Boden lagen,
ich meine die ganze Menschheit,
und darüber nachdachten,
wie der andere da, der auf dem Thron,
zum Verstummen gebracht werden kann?

Und heute sitzen wir alle auf Stühlen,
ich meine die ganze Menschheit,
und denken darüber nach,
woher die Angst kommt, eine Geschichte
zu haben, die sich erzählen läßt,
ohne innezuhalten.

DIE RÜCKKEHR

Die Fliege vorhin,
die über den Küchentisch torkelte,
als mü.te sie sich erholen
von einer großen Müdigkeit.
Zwischen den Krümeln vom Frühstück
las sie das Übriggebliebene,
den verdorbenen Rest.
Menschen, die über Abfallhalden wandern

und alles von uns wissen. Alles.

Sie kennen nicht das Gelübde der Armut.

Später, schon bei den Büchern,

sah ich, wie sie den eigenen Weg

zurückverfolgte und starb.

WEIßDORN

Genug jetzt geschwärmt von den Sonnenuntergängen,

wenn über dem See die Luft so leicht wird,

daß sie den Schmetterling nicht halten kann.

Genug von den Krähen, die in den Pfützen herumstehen

wie Leute, die nicht wissen, was sie mit ihrem Geld

anfangen sollen. Nie wieder erwähnen:

die Förmlichkeit der Tulpen, das rostige Rot

der Flechten und das Gelb abgestorbener Moose,

die Farbe der Rinde der Eiche bei Regen

und Weidenstrünke, die ihre Fäuste recken.

Davon nichts mehr.

Was kostet der Unterhalt einer Seele, natürlich

inflationsbereinigt, dafür bar auf die Hand?

Oder ist alles umsonst?

Sieh, wie der Weißdorn sich aufdrängt!

SONNENBLUMEN UND GEDICHTE

Schau, wie der Himmel sich wölbt
über den mißmutigen Menschen,
die, in ihr Stück Erde verkrallt,
den Blick abwenden vom Licht,
während die Sonnenblumen,
ohne den grauen Hals zu verrenken,
sich um die eigene Achse drehn,
um den letzten Strahl einzufangen.
Es gibt eine Art von Gedichten,
hinter denen man sich verstecken kann,
und andre, die einen zeigen.
Der Spiegel, der am Schuppen hängt,
ist untreu geworden nach vielen Jahren:

Er sammelt das Licht nicht mehr ein,
mit dem ich mir Ausdruck verschaffe.
Wenn es so weitergeht,
wird bald geerntet, Öl und Gedichte.

DAS LEBEN EIN TRAUM

Ich will nicht mehr träumen,
seit sich Nacht für Nacht das Zimmer füllt
mit Menschen, die einmal flüchtig
meinen Weg gekreuzt haben.
Meinen Weg, wie das schon klingt –
ein paar Kiesel, über die ich nicht gestolpert bin.
Sie stehen um mich herum und glotzen,
als hätte ich ihnen mein Leben vorenthalten.
Nun sag schon! Spuck's aus!
Seit ich nicht mehr schlafe,
kommen immer mehr.
Sie schreiben auf, was ich sage,
und schicken es mir zu, eingeschrieben.
Ich lese. Und verstehe nichts mehr.
Soll das mein Leben sein?

DAS BÖSE

In der Stadt heute, in der Sekunde,
da man keinen Schatten wirft,
stand plötzlich das Böse vor mir.
Endlich einmal Auge in Auge!
Ein Wind, zufällig unterwegs wie ich,
blies mir Staub in die Augen,

und als ich sie wieder öffnete,
sprang mir mein Schatten voran.
Ich hatte die Hand noch erhoben,
so daß ich den Teufel an die Wand
malen konnte, wie Kinder es tun.

DER STREIT

Der Streit hatte zwei Hände,
die sich nicht lösen wollten.
So wurde aus einem Abschied
ein Bleiben. Die Hoffnung blieb
trocken unterm Regenschirm.

DER MANN AUS DEM EIBISWALD

Ich lebe hier in diesem Haus,
ich bin hier geboren und werde
hoffentlich auch hier sterben.
Manchmal frage ich mich,
wie die Zeit vergeht.
Ich spreche gerne mit ihr,
aber sie will weiter, weiter.
Meine Lieblingsfarbe ist Grün.
Die Jacke, die Rahmung der Tür,

der Fußabtreter, die Gummischuhe,

alles grün, auch der Regenschirm.

Wie viele unterschiedliche Grüns

gibt es auf unserer Welt?

Früher liebte ich alle Farben,

wie man an dem Flickerlteppich sieht,

der auf der Bank liegt:

alles Stoff von mir.

Ich weiß, daß ich lebe,

aber ich kann es nicht erklären.

Manchmal, wenn ich hier sitze

auf meiner Bank,

läuft ein unglücklicher Schatten

über die Wand, weil die Zeit

nicht stillstehen will, wo doch sonst

alles bei sich selber ist.

EKLEKTISCH, ABER WAHR

Wenn ich nachts auf meiner Terrasse sitze,

der gestirnte Himmel über mir

und die Sprache, die nicht Gesetz werden will,

unter der Zunge, sehe ich, voller Mißtrauen,

zu den säbelrasselnden Sternen hinauf,

die unseren Kalten Krieg überwachen.

Manche der zwanzig Millionen oder mehr,
die wie ich aus ihren Türen treten,
den sich wärmenden Schlüssel
noch in der Hand, geben sich preis,
andere stehen stumm rauchend
auf staunender Erde und frieren.

Aber keiner weiß, was er machen soll
in dieser sternenklaren Nacht,
die uns am Leben hält.

HAUS AM STADTRAND

Frau Sorge hat sich ein Haus gebaut,
am Stadtrand, wo man nicht weiß,
wohin man gehört.
Das Haus hat keine Fenster.
Sie lebt dort mit zwei alten Tugenden,
Geduld und Dankbarkeit,
die ihr abends die Karten legen,
und einem zahnlosen Hund.
Der Narr macht die Einkäufe,
Glühbirnen, Draht, Pflaster gegen die Gicht.
Manchmal kommt ein Greis vorbei,
der hilft ihr im Garten, man hört
seine Gelenke knacken, wenn er sich bückt.

Die Gurken von Frau Sorge, sagt er,

schmecken nach Gurke, als wäre das

eine Wahrheit, die zu sagen sich lohnt.

Frau Sorge hat lange keiner gesehn,

und manche fragen sich,

ob sie überhaupt noch lebt.

TRÄUMEREI

Nichts zu erwarten,

weil der Himmel schon stumm ist

und das Land sich krümmt

in Geduld.

Gesetze auslegen, verändern,

um den Stand der Sonne

zu korrigieren, alles

soll sich ändern,

bis das Warten sich lohnt.

Nur die Stimme verbrennt,

die das Sagen hatte,

den erkennbaren Ton.

Wir wollen die Toten ehren,

die Hüter des Gestern.

Nimm den Staub mit,

denn sie lieben den Staub,

den Staub gib zur Asche,

aus der alles wächst,

was uns hält –

ohne sie wären wir nichts.

TÄGLICHE ÜBUNG

für Friedmar Apel

Wie ein Schüler sitze ich

vor meinem Baum, dem Lehrer.

Eine Stunde hat zwölf Sekunden.

Er unterrichtet mich

in Schattenkunde, Schweigen,

was es heißt, aufrecht zu sein.

Kommt ein Wind auf,

ist die Schule zu Ende,

dann beginnt die Arbeit.

Unter meinem Baum

ist die Schönheit versteckt,

graben ist sinnlos: Man sieht sie

nicht, man muß sie erzählen.

Ein Specht schreibt Zeugnisse:

Schon wieder durchgefallen,

Gott sei Dank!

ZUTRITT VERBOTEN

Unrast heißt das Dorf, in dem ich lebe.

Im Supermarkt gibt es eine eisige Substanz,

die durch den Körper sickert

und in der Erde verschwindet,

ohne daß man sie nachweisen kann.

Sie kostet alles, was du bist.

Die Menschen in meinem Dorf

tragen alte Prophetenmäntel,

außen Wolf, innen Schaf,

das ist gut für die Seele.

Eine Dachrinne, die tropft, ersetzt uns

die Uhr, viel Zeit haben wir nicht.

Aus Hahnenklee und Kornblume

bereiten wir unseren täglichen Tee.

Wenn das Fieber fällt,

lassen die Blumen den Kopf sinken,

dann ist Zeit, mit den Steinen zu reden,

die hier die Verantwortung tragen,

als wäre das ein Beruf.

GUTE VORSÄTZE

Es dämmert, ich habe noch eine Stunde,
dem Tageslicht aus eigener Kraft
ein paar Zeilen zu opfern. Es ist so ruhig,
daß man die Dinge flüstern hört.
Das Elend wächst in der Ferne, wo ich,
an die Nähe gefesselt, nicht bin,
aber sein wollte, als ich jung war.
Es wächst geduldiger, als man denken kann.
Jetzt Pläne machen für die Zeit davor,
um der Sache, die wir Leben nennen,
doch noch eine Richtung zu geben,
eine schöne, das wär's.
Aber die Tiefe reizt mich nicht,
solange ich den Vögeln zuschauen kann,
die ohne Kummer und ohne Tränen
in diesem späten Licht ein Haus skizzieren,
in dem sich leben läßt,
ein Haus für Pilger ohne Bitterkeit.

DER ANDERE GOTT

Wenn man, ganz unerwartet, so alt wird wie ich,
träumt man immer häufiger von einem Land
ohne den Schabernack, der uns als Leben

verkauft wird: von einer anderen Erzählung.

Auch die Geschichte mit Gott muß anders erzählt werden.

Die Vorstellung zum Beispiel, daß hinter unserem Gott

noch ein anderer Gott steht, der ihn beaufsichtigt,

ist beunruhigend. Beaufsichtigen trifft die Sache

vielleicht nicht oder nicht ganz. Es geht darum,

daß unser Gott zu lange in der Hoffnung lebte,

nicht durchschaut zu werden. Da aber alle Menschen

etwas zu fürchten haben müssen, sollte ihnen

nicht immer vergeben werden, das ist wahr.

Mit diesen Gedanken saß ich unter dem Baum

und schaute zu, wie die Tage ins Land gingen,

mal allmählich, dann wieder plötzlich,

als hätten sie es eilig, von meinen Gedanken wegzukommen.

DIE FLIEGE

Als ich heute, offenen Auges, der Fliege

gefolgt bin, die mit nimmermüder Geduld

jeden Zentimeter des Fensters beschrieb,

hinter dem der Frühling begann sich zu strecken,

dachte ich, daß ihr wirres Serifengekrakel

von der anderen Seite gelesen werden könnte

als ein großes Gedicht über den Trost

des Scheiterns in einer zu großzügigen Welt.

Irgendwann, mitten im gebrochenen Vers,

fiel sie auf die Fensterbank und zappelte

mit den Beinchen, als wollte sie,

vor dem Ende, ihr Werk noch vollenden,

das unvollendet blieb. Dann die Dämmerung,

die mit rosaroter Geste das Fenster reinigte,

weil ein Leben, das nichts verspricht,

keinen Endreim haben darf vor dem Tod.

WIE ICH DIE NACHT VERBRACHTE

Wo soll die andre Welt beginnen,

das fremde Gebiet, in dem die sachlichen Stimmen

keinen Widerstand finden und einfach aufgeben,

so wie wir alle irgendwann aufgeben, wenn der Abend

sich hinzieht und die Not keinen Ausweg kennt?

Wir werden nie vernünftig, das ist das Gebot,

das wissen die Heimchen und die Glühwürmchen,

die mit Freude ihre Batterien leeren.

Dieser Baum am See, ein Obdach für mich

für eine lange Nacht, gebettet auf Leberblümchen

und Brennesseln, die nach dumpfer Hitze riechen.

Ich höre, wie die Fledermäuse das Wasser ritzen

und die Fische zwingen, das Element zu wechseln.

Und wäre nicht der schrille Schrei gewesen

eines Nachtvogels, wie aus der Stille geschnitten,

ich hätte den Glauben verloren für immer.

NÄHE

Vor meinem Bett
steht ein Löwe.
Er muß in der Nähe
leben, denn er kommt
regelmäßig vorbei,
einmal im Monat.
Wenn er da ist,
schlafe ich ruhig.
Kein böser Traum
traut sich in seine
Nähe.

TRÄUMEREI

Auf Matratzen, wahllos
im Raum verstreut,
sitzt der Kummer.
Eine Flasche Wein kreist.
Draußen fahren Schiffe vorbei,
die nicht ankern können.
Wir hören unser Herz,
bevor es zerspringt
in der Stille.

15. MAI

Ich habe ein kleines Feuer gemacht
im Garten, um einen Halt zu finden
in den Flammen, aber es will nicht brennen.
Die Augen folgen den Rauchwolken,
die sich aus der Asche quälen
und den Nußbaum kitzeln, den Neinsager.
Wie soll man behalten,
was einem das Gras erzählt?
Der Specht jedenfalls stottert,
wenn er Trost schreiben soll,
dieses schöne einsilbige Wort
mit fünf Buchstaben.
Unrast heißt ein Dorf in der Nähe,
da leben bewaffnete Schatten,
alle Umwege führen zu ihm hin.
Ich will die Gabe erlernen,
nicht zu vergessen,
was das Beste im Leben ist,
aber Gaben kann man nicht erlernen.

NICHTS, WAS WIR SCHON KENNEN

Davon leben wir, wenn das Gewitter vorbei ist
und wir ein Teil des Bodens werden dürfen;
wenn Tag und Nacht sich endlich erschließen,
um uns wieder einzulassen;
wenn ein Licht über den Dingen liegt
wie ein Tuch, das den Schwalben entglitt;
wenn aus dem Riß im Geweb
die Lerche aufsteigt und den Himmel reizt;
wenn der Specht mit dem bösen Blick
sein monotones Wir können über alles reden
den Buchen diktiert, die das Mögliche hüten
in dem kühlen Raum zu ihren Fü.en.
Nichts, was wir schon kennen, davon leben wir.

Einsicht, Unterscheidung, Freude und Gedächtnis,
so stand's im Testament, sollen uns gehören,
aber nur, wenn wir Kinder bleiben, die der Welt
auf den Wecker gehen, bevor es klingelt.

ZUR PHILOSOPHIE

Wir müssen davon ausgehen,
daß Voraussagen nicht eintreffen,
etwas geht immer schief. Immer.
Auf den Menschen ist kein Verlaß,
deshalb sind wir noch am Leben.
Einer schaut aus dem Fenster
und blickt einem Hund hinterher,
der andere bewundert das Licht
auf den hellen Blättern der Linde.
Zu viele sind bei sich, also nicht
bei der Sache. Wir haben eine Ahnung
von unseren Grenzen, mehr nicht.
Die Geschichte, sagt ein Freund,
ist die Wissenschaft vom Unglück
des Menschen, von Leopardi bis Cioran.
Die Poetik des Unvollendeten,
die feste Verbindung von Philosophie und Trauer,
daran wollen wir arbeiten, denn:
der Mensch ist ein zögerndes Wesen –
oder nicht?
Komm, laß uns gehen, das Gehen
hilft uns, das Geläufige zu verstehen,
ohne daß wir es übersetzen müssen.

WAHLSONNTAG

Nichts Neues von den Wolken

zu sagen, der stummen Begleitung,

sie scheinen zu rasten über dem Land.

Nicht Frieden mehr und noch nicht Krieg,

das weiß auch die Spinne, bis gestern

in der Hecke weitmaschig beschäftigt

mit der Geschichte des Sommers,

jetzt sitzt sie im Eck des Fensters

und wartet auf Sonne.

Keine Schmetterlinge mehr,

die mir das Blut stocken lassen im Herzen.

Und der Apfelbaum? Zuckt manchmal

mit den Schultern, als schämte er sich,

in diesem Jahr keinen einzigen Apfel

werfen zu können ins trübe Grün des Rasens.

Immer deutscher sieht er aus

im Alter. Nichts Neues seit Goethe

von den Wolken zu sagen,

sie hängen über dem Land,

in dem die Unfreiheit der Freiheit

an den Kragen will, wie es heißt

auf den Plakaten, die morgen endlich

wieder weggeschafft werden,

um Platz zu machen für den freien Blick

ins dunkle Land.

OFFENE FENSTER

Manche hocken, Rücken an Rücken

mit ihren glanzlosen Büchern,

und sinnen auf Rache.

Der Abend zieht vorbei,

er sammelt die Toten einfach ein

bei offenen Fenstern.

Alles, was wir sehen,

bekommt einen Namen.

Auch die Sterne,

die unter Lichtschwäche leiden.

Sie halten sich streng

an die Bahn des Kometen,

den Pilgerpfad,

der vor einem schimmernden Haufen

endet: den Plejaden.

Nur hier,

in diesem Staat im Staate, geht es namenlos zu.

Auch der Mond,

durch ein unzertrennliches Schicksal

an uns gekettet,

kann uns nicht helfen.

Er besitzt keinen biologischen Wert.

Von seinen Sternen umgeben,

ist er das Ideal der Unverwandelbarkeit.

Ein kalter König in einem verkabelten Reich.

Kratergebirge, der Boden durchlöchert

wie ein Sieb.

Von seiner Höhe aus

wird das Leben etwas weniger wichtig,

sagen alle, die in seinem Licht

nach Hause kommen,

trockenen Fußes, weil er der Erde

das Wasser entzieht.

BEOBACHTUNG

Jemand hat seinen Namen
in die Wolke gemeißelt
über meinem Haus
mit blutigen Händen.
Alles, was vorbeifährt,
wird rot.
Schnell die Fenster schließen,
damit die Farbe im Haus bleibt,
die nicht rot ist.
Und bitte nicht lesen wollen.

REQUIEM FÜR EINEN WIND

Noch standen hier die Worte,
verlegen zwar und voller Scham,
und hier und da war eines schon gebrochen.
Die Welt zu klein für ihren Anspruch,
für einen neuen großen Anfang.
Die Welt will andre Worte haben,
seitdem das helle Staunen sich
im freien Fall befindet und nicht
die alten schönen Worte braucht,
die dumme Unersättlichkeit zu feiern.
Dann kam ein Wind auf, unerwartet,

der uns nicht mehr schlafen ließ,

der hatte sich vom Krieg ernährt,

von tausend Traurigkeiten,

und ließ das falsche Elend tanzen.

Vor Tag noch war's vorbei.

Und tief erschrocken sammelte die Kunst

den Mangel ein, für den es keine Sprache gab.

Nur Bilder.

IM WALD

Bisweilen erscheint es uns so,

als könnten wir unser Leben

noch führen, auf ein Ziel zu,

das nicht der Tod ist, sondern etwas davor,

das zwar in Wurzelverwandtschaft

mit ihm steht, aber sich vor ihm

verzweigt in größter Pedanterie.

Der Regen hat plötzlich aufgehört,

aber es tropft noch lange von den Bäumen,

und wenn man einfach stehenbliebe,

wie angewurzelt, würde man wissen,

was noch zu tun ist: wenig,

viel oder gar das Entscheidende?

Aber man will weiter, auch wenn man

nicht gezwungen ist, das Leben zu lieben,

und plötzlich die Tropfen zählt,

wie sie fallen auf den feuchten Grund.

Der Wald gibt sich Mühe, auszusehen

wie ein Bild aus dem 19. Jahrhundert,

auf dem Menschen verboten sind.

Das Inventar des Himmels ist leer,

die Sterne alle kassiert.

Ich wollte dem Kind eine Sternschnuppe

zeigen, das schönste geräuschlose Spiel,

das ein müder Gott sich erfand.

Vielleicht brauchen wir nichts zu wünschen?

Vielleicht leben wir schon im Paradies?

NOTIZBUCH

In sein Notizbuch schrieb er:

Wie zufrieden die Überlebenden sind!

Sie haben der Zukunft den Schmerz genommen,

dem Honig die Sü.e, der Distel den Stachel.

Das Leid lebt gut in festen Häusern,

wir hören es rumpeln in der Nacht.

Es überlebte ein Lärm ohne Stille,

der steht überm Marktplatz und schreit.

IV

Verpaßte Gelegenheiten

Für Manfred Trojahn

1

Wie sie da so stand, erzählte einer aus Rom,

an die Mauer gelehnt, mit Augen,

aus denen das Glück schon geschwunden war,

so wunderbar träge wie ein Tag

im späten Sommer und so unzugänglich

wie die gesch.ftstüchtigen kleinen Götter,

die am Pantheon die Zeit totschlagen,

die Zeit, die nichts von Menschen wissen will,

und wie sie ihre rechte Hand zum Kopf führte,

so langsam, als wäre die Luft zäher Sirup,

und ihr Gesicht berührte, eine staubige Landschaft

aus trockenen Äckern und versiegten Brunnen,

zu der Stunde, da der Tag sich schließlich

vom Schatten trennt und die Geräusche der Stadt

noch einmal aufdrehen, war ich mir plötzlich sicher,

daß sie es ist, auf die alle gewartet haben

am Ende einer langen Gegenwart,

die nicht vergehen will.

2

Ich saß im Café, sagt eine, allein,

in der Nähe von Ostia, direkt am Meer,

um die lange Weile nach dem Glück zu genießen,

und las deine Postkarten, bis an den Rand gefüllt

mit deinen untreuen Worten. Ein Schiff legte ab, von Möwen

mit Geschrei aus dem Hafen geleitet, das nahm

meine Erinnerungen mit und ließ mich leer zurück,

unermeßlich leer – bis auf die Kindheit, die wollte nicht

mitreisen: der Geruch nach überreifen Feigen,

streunende Liebe, Ungenügen, das alles blieb bei mir.

Die Brücke vom Wollen zum Handeln zerstört.

Gestern noch dachte ich, diese Postkarten von dir,

das langt für mein Leben, dieser z.hflüssige Kitsch,

der fester ist als alle großen Bekenntnisse.

Einer saß in der Nähe, zwei Tische weiter,

der kam mir bekannt vor, aber nicht genug,

um mein Gedächtnis zu reizen. Sein flaches Gesicht

ein unbeschriebenes Blatt, frei für ein offenes Wort.

3

An einem dieser hohlwangigen Tage

im November in Berlin, sagte er,

wenn die Sonnenuhr nur bis drei zählen kann

und die Stadt zu schlafen versucht

unter der Nebeldecke, saß ich im Bus,

der den Kurfürstendamm hinunterkroch

auf der Überholspur, deren Belag glitzerte

wie eine Landebahn aus zerbrochenen Flaschen.

Schlüter-, Bleibtreu-, Fasanenstraße,

die vertrauten Ecken, Benjamin-Land,

jetzt zugestellt mit Mode und Fast Food,

damit, wenn das Unglück es will, Wünsche

in Erfüllung gehen. Da sah ich sie,

gehüllt in einen Regenmantel, im Rücken gebauscht,

ihr hageres Gesicht, wie von Käthe Kollwitz gezeichnet,

über einen Stadtplan gebeugt, auf dem sie

den Horizont suchte, den wir, noch als Schüler,

in dieser gußeisernen Gegend vermuteten.

4

Es begann zu regnen, sagte sie,

und das in Hannover, wenn Sie wissen, was ich meine.

Ich saß in dem Hotel gegenüber vom Bahnhof

und schaute auf die ungläubigen Bäume,

die sich so ungeschickt verneigten, als hätten sie Schmerzen.

Neben mir in der Lobby, auf einem häßlichen Stühlchen,

saß ein Lümmel, im Mantel, und fragte seine Großmutter:

Na, hat sich dein Leben gelohnt? Und sah mich verblüfft

dabei an, als könnte er selbst nicht glauben,

Urheber dieser Geschmacklosigkeit zu sein. Sitzt da

wie sein Vater, dachte ich, der ihm die Blödheit vererbt hat.

Gerade war ich dabei, ihm mit meinem heißen Kaffee

den Tag zu verderben, als er draußen vorbeiging, der,

auf den ich gewartet hatte, dessentwegen ich

zum ersten Mal in meinem Leben nach Hannover gefahren war.

Merkwürdig sah er aus, zuviel Seele für seinen Körper,

ärmlich. Auf jeden Fall, dachte ich, als er ins Taxi stieg,

hätte ich die gesamte Rechnung bezahlen müssen.

5

Eine Konferenz zwang mich, nach Warschau zu reisen,

klagte er, obwohl ich Lissabon vorgezogen hätte,

noch dazu am Jahrestag des Erdbebens.

Wir hatten uns vor dem Schloß verabredet,

keine wirklich gute Idee, weil zehntausend Paare

sich versammelt hatten in ihrem Glück

und sich nicht trennen wollten, auf keinen Fall.

Es hätte schlimmer kommen können, sagte ich mir

zwischen zwei Phasen der Niedergeschlagenheit,

weil ich dich partout nicht finden konnte.

In der nächstbesten Kirche entzündete ich eine Kerze,

eine nur, um einerseits Maria nicht zu verwöhnen

und um andererseits den Tod nicht zu reizen,

der anwesend war. Mir fiel, kniend in der Bank, ein,

daß ich an dich wie an eine Verstorbene dachte,

ich sah dein unstetes Gesicht erstarrt zu einer Maske.

Ich war an dem Punkt angekommen, wo das Leben

in mir zurückkriechen wollte in die Leblosigkeit.

6

In dem Hotel gegenüber der Kathedrale
von Barcelona, sagte sie, hatte ich ganz oben
ein Zimmer genommen, um auf dich zu warten.
Auf dem gesprungenen Spiegel versuchte eine Fliege,
die nicht wußte, daß sie am Abend tot sein würde,
mir die Zukunft zu lesen und gab auf.
Auch der Spiegel erkannte mich nicht wieder.
Auf den Treppen der Kathedrale, in heller Sonne,
beteten die Ungläubigen und stritten um eine Münze,
die ein Vogel verloren hatte, einer dieser Vögel,
die seit Jahrhunderten versuchen, die Kathedrale
in den Himmel zu heben. Aus dem Gully kam Rauch,
wahrscheinlich wurde unten Zurbarans Lamm gebraten,
daneben schüttete ein alter Mann sein Herz aus
vor den aufgeregten Spatzen. Eine Ameisenstraße
lief über den Balkon, sie mußte sich verirrt haben.
Dann sah ich dich aus dem Gotteshaus treten
und in der Menge verschwinden.

7

Keine Ahnung, warum wir uns ausgerechnet
in Stockholm treffen sollten, im Februar,
wenn man die Hand nicht vor den Augen sieht,
aber sie bestand auf einem ›kalten‹ Gespräch.
Drei Tage saß ich in meinem Hotelzimmer
und sah dem Schnee zu, wie er sich restlos
im Hafenbecken auflöste. Die Lage des Menschen
ist ungewiß, waren ihre letzten Worte am Telefon,
aber wir haben gute Aussichten zu überleben.
Sie liebte die Idee von der Befristung der Welt.
Am vierten Tag blieb ich in einer Demo kleben,
vor dem Kulturhaus. Wenn sie in der Stadt wäre,
würde ich sie hier finden, obwohl ich nicht sicher war,
ob ich sie erkennen würde, zu oft hatten wir uns
verpaßt. In der Nacht sah ich im TV eine Reportage
über die Demonstration, ich verstand nicht,
um was es ging. Aber ich sah mich in der Menge
und hinter mir, mit aufgerissenem Mund, sie.

8

Es gehörte zu seinen verrückten Ideen,

daß wir uns im Nachtzug nach Venedig treffen sollten.

Ich stieg in München ein und ging in den Speisewagen,

damit er mich sehen konnte. Ein Platz war noch frei.

Einem Sack voll Blut saß ich gegenüber, der Karten legte,

um sein Schicksal zu ergründen, das ihm nur allzu deutlich

im Gesicht stand. Eine Büffelherde raste im Dunkel an uns vorbei,

ich konnte ihr Keuchen hören; sie folgte einem Falter,

der ihr alle Grenzen öffnete. Von ihm, der auf mich warten wollte,

war nichts zu sehen. In Österreich verließen die Betten den Zug,

sie wurden woanders gebraucht, und nahmen die Träume mit.

Wir mußten im Stehen schlafen wie heimatlose Gedanken.

Jedes Wort, das mir durch den Kopf ging, baute mit

an der Mauer, die uns trennte. Es ist alles gesagt worden über Venedig.

Auf dem Rückweg sah ich ihn auf einem Vaporetto,

der uns entgegenkam, sein Haar wehte mächtig im Wind.

Wie Münzen schnippte er seine Jahre ins Wasser

und schaute nicht einmal aus den Augenwinkeln zu mir her.

9

Zum zehnten Jahrestag unseres Verpassens
wollten wir uns in Saint Germain treffen, im Flore.
Ich war früh dran, um aus dem hintersten Eck
der Veranda ihr Kommen zu beobachten,
wie sie sich zwischen Wölfen und Schafen
einen Weg bahnt. Europa trank teuren Kaffee,
als wäre nichts passiert. Die gemeinsame Erde,
las ich, die keine Gemeinsamkeit mehr kennt,
wird großmäulig vor die Hunde gehen. Nur wir
werden überleben, zusammen mit dieser Fliege,
die sich ungeniert auf meinem Teller putzte.
Sei unbesorgt, flüsterte ich, ich halte zu dir.
Da sah ich sie. Sie stand auf der anderen Seite
der Straße und schien zu überlegen, ob es sich lohne.
Ein Bettler hielt ihr die Hand hin, und sie
kramte lange in den Taschen ihres Mantels
nach einer Münze, die sie ihm so ungeschickt gab,
daß sie zur Erde fiel. Dann war sie verschwunden.

10

Und schließlich Sils-Maria, das war unvermeidlich.

Es war im Juni, sagte sie, und man konnte spüren,

wie sich die Welt gegen die Verwandlung wehrte.

Der gregorianische Gesang der fallenden Tropfen,

und auf dem Stein für Nietzsche ein erster schüchterner Falter

mit zusammengebissenen Flügeln, der wollte nicht

auffliegen vor der Zeit. Hier saß ich, wartend, wartend,

auf nichts. Jenseits von gut und böse, bald

des Lichts genießend, bald des Schattens,

ganz nur Spiel, ganz See, ganz Mittag, ganz Zeit

ohne Ziel. Aber keiner kam die Berge herab.

Im Waldhaus, in der Chasté kein Gast,

der ihm ähnlich sah, kein Fußabdruck im Schlamm,

nur dieser Falter, der ihn gesehen haben muß.

Ein hinkender Vogel ging vorbei, erhobenen Hauptes,

und auf dem See Enten, glänzend wie Ebenholz.

Gelegentlich hörte ich flüsternde Stimmen,

die mich durchfuhren wie ein Messer das Brot.

Ich war nicht erstaunt, daß sie mich in Jerusalem treffen wollte,

sie liebte Klischees und Steine. Es wird kommen der Tag, da die Steine

zu uns sprechen werden, war eine ihrer Redensarten,

sie schwärmte von den lichten Schatten der Tamarisken,

von den feierlichen Eseln vor dem Tor des Erbarmens,

beladen mit einer Bürde, alt wie die Geschichte der Menschheit,

von einem Messias aus Honig, mit einer Krone aus den Nadeln der Pinie,

von einem Gott, der die Schlüssel verlor zu seiner Schöpfung.

Ich fragte bei der American Colony nach ihr, auch im King David

kannte keiner ihren Namen, kein Bett ihren Körper. Durch alle Kirchen

war ich geschlichen wie eine Katze, hatte mich dem Singsang

aller Sprachen ergeben, die hier geboren wurden im Sand, den Gebeten

und Rufen und dem Gelächter der Vögel, die wie Drohnen kreisten

über den geweihten Stätten und den verirrten Seelen am Abend.

Da sah ich sie. Sie stand im Hof der Armenischen Kathedrale,

wo der zerfressene Schädel des Apostels Jakobus aufbewahrt wird.

Sie stand, eingehüllt in einen weißen Schal, mit einem Priester im Schatten,

der dichter und dichter wurde, bis endlich der Shabbath begann.

Es war schwerer als gedacht, ihn wiederzufinden, sagte sie.

Erst füllte der Schnee seine gut sichtbaren Spuren,

dann ein lustloser Regen, schließlich setzte der Wind

unseren Wegen zu, die nur in weitem Abstand noch

zu sehen waren. Gelegentlich fand ich ein Foto von ihm

in der Zeitung, schwarzweiß sein bedrücktes Gesicht,

ein Panorama des Elends. In den Städten begegnete ich

manchmal seinem Schatten, der sich aufbäumte vor mir,

also mußte er hinter mir her sein. Und ich hörte ihn,

da war es schon Frühjahr, durch das alte Laub schlurfen,

die übriggebliebenen Blätter, wie ein störrisches Kind,

das die Fü.e nicht mehr heben will. Und dann fand ich

einen Zettel von ihm, in Schönschrift beschrieben,

unter einem leeren Weinglas: Bin gleich zurück. Bitte warte

nicht. Das war in Skopje, in einem dieser lauten Cafés

hinter dem Pferd Alexanders des Großen,

in denen man nicht merkt, daß die Zeit einen narrt.

Aber sie narrte uns beide, ihn und natürlich auch mich.

13

Ich mußte lernen, an ihr vorbeizugehen,

ohne zu stolpern, ihren Blick nicht zu erwidern.

Manchmal sah ich sie in einem Café sitzen,

ein Buch vor sich, mit dem sie spielte,

als hätte es ihr nichts mehr zu sagen

oder als hätte es seine Stimme verloren.

Heruntergekommen sah sie aus, lebensmüd,

nur die Schuhe immer tipptopp geputzt,

sie sollten, sagte sie manchmal, den Tod ertragen.

Nur ertragen, natürlich, nicht anerkennen,

denn die Angst vor dem Tod hatte sie ausgestanden.

So konnte ich sie mir auch als Tote vorstellen,

in ihrem Gesicht ein letztes waches Träumen,

schon eingehüllt von der Nacht der Welt.

Die letzten Worte müssen die Augen sprechen,

das langsame Wehe, wie in Honig getaucht.

An einem unauffindbaren Ort werden wir uns treffen,

sagte sie, wo unsere Stimme auf uns wartet.

Der Zyklus »Verpaßte Gelegenheiten« wurde auf Anregung von Franz Xaver Ohnesorg geschrieben und von Manfred Trojahn (wunderbar) vertont. Bei derUraufführung am 16 . Juli 2017 im Lehmbruck Museum in Duisburg spielte die Pianistin Hanni Liang. Allen drei Freunden danke ich von Herzen.